Ultimate!
REPUBLICAN
TRIVIA

1001
Fun and Fascinating Facts

Scott Paul Frush

MARSHALL RAND PUBLISHING
Royal Oak, Michigan

Marshall Rand Publishing

P.O. Box 1849
Royal Oak, Michigan 48068-1849

Printed in the United States of America

Frush, Scott Paul
    Ultimate Republican Trivia / Scott Paul Frush

ISBN 0-9744374-1-7

Library of Congress Control Number: 2008931229

CONTENTS

ABOUT THE AUTHOR

Scott Frush received an MBA from the University of Notre Dame and his bachelor's degree from Eastern Michigan University. He is an assistant vice president for investments and wealth management with a regional Midwest bank located in the suburbs of Detroit.

While in college, Scott joined the Republican National Committee to support and advance the ideals of fiscal responsibility and strong social morals. In addition to the RNC, Scott is a member of the Michigan Republicans, Irish-American Republicans, Detroit Economic Club, CFA Institute, National Italian American Foundation, Knights of Columbus, and Catholic League for Religious and Civil Rights.

Scott in Jackson, Michigan, site of the founding of the Republican Party

Professionally, Scott is a leading authority on asset allocation policy and portfolio optimization. He has helped investors protect, grow, and insure their wealth for well over a decade.

Scott was named the 2007 recipient of *CFA Magazine's* prestigious "Most Investor Oriented" award, which recognizes one CFA Institute member who has made outstanding contributions to investor education. In addition, he was profiled in the July 2008 issue of *Bank Investment Consultant* magazine for his approach to wealth management.

Scott holds the Chartered Financial Analyst (CFA) and Certified Financial Planner (CFP) designations as well as various insurance and securities licenses.

Scott is the author of six other books—five on investments and one on trivia. His latest investing book is titled *Commodities Demystified*, published in July 2008 by McGraw-Hill.

MORE FROM SCOTT

Commodities Demystified
Publication Date: July 31, 2008
Publisher: McGraw-Hill
ISBN: 0071549501
Pages: 304

Hedge Funds Demystified
Publication Date: September 17, 2007
Publisher: McGraw-Hill
▶ Named "Our Editor's Pick" by *Standard & Poor's Financial Communications*; October 2007

Understanding Hedge Funds
Publication Date: December 22, 2006
Publisher: McGraw-Hill
▶ Named "Pick of the Week" by *Notre Dame Magazine*, Spring 2007

Ultimate Italian Trivia
Publication Date: October 9, 2006
Publisher: Marshall Rand Publishing
▶ Financially sponsored by the National Italian American Foundation (NIAF)

Understanding Asset Allocation
Publication Date: September 25, 2006
Publisher: McGraw-Hill
ISBN: 007147594X
Pages: 208

Optimal Investing
Publication Date: April 1, 2004
Publisher: Marshall Rand Publishing
▶ "Book of the Year" 2004 Finalist for Business & Economics by *ForeWord Magazine*

These books are available online at www.Amazon.com

LIST OF FIGURES

INTRODUCTION

Founded in 1854 by anti-slavery expansion activists, the Republican Party named John Fremont its first presidential nominee, but rose to prominence under Abraham Lincoln, the first Republican president. As with any great idea, there is a spark of inspiration that transforms a simple concept into a mighty force. For the founding members of the GOP, a term coined many years later, that spark was opposition to the Kansas-Nebraska Act that would have allowed the expansion of slavery into Kansas. From these early days, the Republican Party has revolutionized politics in America, defended our freedoms, fostered a heightened sense of patriotism, and advanced our pursuit of happiness. The following is a passage from the Republican Creed that exemplifies the principles, character, and spirit of all people proud to call themselves Republicans:

I do not choose to be a common man.
It is my right to be uncommon.

I prefer the challenges of life to
guaranteed security, the thrill of fulfillment
to the state of calm utopia.

I will not trade freedom for beneficence,
nor my dignity for a handout.

Republicans have been very instrumental in shaping of American society in so many ways. The breadth and depth of the Party's influence is quite remarkable with more than 55 million Americans proudly calling themselves Republicans. Among this group are very distinguished luminaries from the fields of politics, business, religion, sports, military, entertainment, law, and the arts. This book will help you to learn and understand many of their accomplishments and contributions.

All of the major periods of Republican Party history are covered in **Ultimate Republican Trivia**, including the early days, the Lincoln era,

Reconstruction, the Gilded Age, the Age of Dominance, the Age of the New Deal, Modern Republicanism, the Reagan era, and the modern era.

Each chapter in this book targets a specific subject and, as a result, presents trivia questions that are related. In addition to the nine chapters, there are appendices with useful non-trivia information. Appendix A provides a list of Republican resources, including organizations and publications. Appendix B provides a list of notable Republicans, including presidents, vice-presidents, and first ladies. In addition, included in the chapters are historical photographs of Republicans and landmarks. Also included are "Republican Top 10" lists, "It Happened On…" event profiles, and a timeline of key dates in Republican history at the top of each page.

With *Ultimate Republican Trivia*, my singular aim was to showcase the best of the Republican Party from pioneering politicians to groundbreaking accomplishments. What many readers may find quite surprising is that nowhere in the book will you find the word of the competing political party. The intent is to take the higher ground and highlight what the Republican Party is all about without attacking or demeaning another political party. It's the essence of how Americans wish politicians would act themselves.

It is my sincere desire that *Ultimate Republican Trivia* becomes both your reference guide and source of fun and entertainment. I've planted the seed of discovery and exploration, now I turn it over to you for your reading enjoyment. So join me for a fun and fascinating journey through all things Republican!

- Scott Paul Frush

CHAPTER
O·N·E

ORIGINS, ORGANIZATIONS, & LANDMARKS

The Rise of America's Party

"Fourscore and seven years ago our fathers brought forth on this continent, a new nation, conceived in Liberty, and dedicated to the proposition that all men are created equal."

- ABRAHAM LINCOLN

"We don't need radical new directions—we need strong, steady, experienced leadership."

- GEORGE H. W. BUSH

3/20/1854 ▶ **Anti-slavery activists opposed to the Kansas-Nebraska Act meet in Ripon, Wisconsin.**

---

(1) Many of the initial policies of the Republican Party were inspired by which defunct political party?

(2) The "Republican" Party name was selected to honor an American president who established a political party of like ideals. Name this president.

(3) The chairman of this organization is chosen by the president when the Republicans hold the presidency and is chosen by Republican state committees when the Republicans do not hold the presidency. Name this organization.

(4) If you want to visit the Eisenhower National Historic Site, where would you go?

(5) Founded in 1958 by Robert Welch, this conservative organization attracted followers for its militant anti-Communism and conspireatorial view of the world. Name this organization.

(6) In 1902, President Theodore Roosevelt established a national park in Oregon. Name this national park. (Hint: Lake)

(7) Abraham Lincoln gained national recognition for his debates with which senator in the Illinois senatorial campaign of 1858?

(8) "California White House" was the nickname given to which Republican's elegant San Clemente home?

(9) In 1893, twenty-two clerks were killed when a floor collapsed in this landmark Washington, D.C. structure. Name this structure. (Hint: Lincoln)

7/6-13/1854 ▶ Anti-slavery activists hold a state convention in Jackson, Michigan and take the Republican Party name.

(10) A motif of which famous event can be found on the reverse side of the Eisenhower $1 coin?

(11) What is the name for the well-known Christian organization, established by Pat Robertson, considered one of the most influential right-wing organizations in American politics?

(12) Who was the very first Republican vice president of the United States? (Hint: Maine)

(13) Which American president and his wife are buried in a bird sanctuary named for him in Oyster Bay, New York?

(14) In which Great Lakes city can you find the famous Saint-Gaudens statue of Abraham Lincoln?

(15) In what town was the Republican Party formally established in 1854?

(16) The Indian head penny was replaced by which coin?

(17) Which Republican served as the chairman of the National Republican Committee from 1973 to 1974?

(18) In which city can you find the Gerald R. Ford Library?

Rutherford B. Hayes

(19) After which classical-period structure is the Lincoln Memorial modeled?

(20) Which airport serving the Washington, D.C. area is named for a Republican president?

(21) The National Cathedral in Washington, D.C. showcases two presidential statues, one of George Washington and the other of a Republican president. Name this president.

Ultimate Republican Trivia

6/19/1856 ▶ First Republican National Convention nominates John C. Fremont
for president.

(22) In 1914, former president Theodore Roosevelt nearly died from a severe fever he contracted while exploring a waterway called the River of Doubt, later renamed Rio Roosevelt in honor of Roosevelt. In which country is this waterway located?

(23) Which Republican president is buried in Lake View Cemetery in Cleveland, Ohio?

(24) Established in 1938 by Marion E. Martin, this Republican organization was founded to educate, inform and motivate women to become political activists. Name this organization with nearly 2,000 chapters located throughout the United States, Puerto Rico, and the Virgin Islands.

(25) The Theodore Roosevelt National Memorial Park, the only national park named for an American president, is located in which state?

(26) What is the name of the pool, approximately 2,029 feet long and 167 feet wide, leading to the steps of the Lincoln Memorial?

(27) In which city can you find a large park named for Ulysses S. Grant? (Hint: Buckingham Fountain)

(28) In which city can you find the Gerald R. Ford International Airport?

(29) What rights do Log Cabin Republicans advocate?

(30) Which Republican presidential library and museum, operated by the Forbes Library, is located in Northampton, Massachusetts?

(31) According to the Oxford English Dictionary, when was the first known reference to the Republican Party as the "Grand Old Party"? (a) 1854, (b) 1876, (c) 1924, (d) 1946

(32) In which city can you visit the Benjamin Harrison Memorial Home?

(33) This symbol was the traditional symbol of the Republican Party in many Midwestern states in the early 20th century and still appears on Indiana ballots. What is this symbol?

11/4/1856 ▶ Republicans win 92 seats in the U.S. House of Representatives in the 1856 election.

(34) In 1856, this famous explorer, soldier, and California senator ran as the first Republican nominee for president using the political slogan, "Free soil, free labor, free speech, free men...." Name this Republican defeated by James Buchanan.

(35) The Lincoln Memorial in Washington, D.C. contains 36 Doric columns. What do these columns symbolize?

(36) Abraham Lincoln owned only one home in his life time. Where can you find this home today?

> **IT HAPPENED ON SEPTEMBER 8, 1954**
>
> ▶ President Dwight D. Eisenhower signs the bill that authorizes the joint U.S.-Canada building of the St. Lawrence Seaway, one of the most complex inland navigation systems in the world. Queen Elizabeth and Eisenhower dedicate the Seaway five years later.

(37) The Lincoln Memorial in Washington, D.C. contains inscriptions of two speeches made by Abraham Lincoln. Name these two speeches.

(38) United States Supreme Court Chief Justice William H. Taft dedicated which memorial in Washington, D.C. in 1922?

(39) What is the largest mausoleum in North America?

(40) The primary mission of this federal agency, established by President George W. Bush, is to help prevent, protect against, and respond to acts of terrorism on United States soil. Name this federal agency.

(41) Grant's Farm, a 281-acre wildlife preserve and historical home of Ulysses S. Grant, is presently the country estate of the Busch family (as in Anheuser-Busch). Near which city can you find the home Grant dubbed "Hardscrabble Farm"?

(42) In which western state can you find a mountain range named in honor of Ulysses S. Grant?

(43) This state maintains its Old State Capitol in the same condition as it was during the life of Abraham Lincoln. Name this state.

5/15/1860 ▶ Abraham Lincoln is nominated for president at the Republican National Convention in Chicago.

REPUBLICAN TOP 10

Most Vetoes by a Republican President

	PRESIDENT	VETOES
1	Dwight D. Eisenhower	181
2	Ulysses S. Grant	93
3	Theodore Roosevelt	82
4	Ronald Reagan	78
5	Gerald Ford	66
6	Calvin Coolidge	50
7	Benjamin Harrison	44
8	George H. W. Bush	44
9	Richard Nixon	43
10	William McKinley	42

(44) For which Republican president is the Library of Congress' concert hall named?

(45) What class of ship is the U.S.S. *Ronald Reagan* (CVN-76)?

(46) According to the National Federation of Republican Women, what percentage of state legislators in 2008 are women? (a) 5%, (b) 19%, (c) 24%, (d) 38%

(47) On the campus of which university is the George Bush Presidential Library and Museum located?

(48) This organization is charged with the responsibility of promoting Republican campaign activities, developing and promoting the Republican political platform, coordinating fundraising, and developing election strategy. Name this organization.

(49) In which town can you find the Eisenhower Center, a complex consisting of a library, museum, family home, and burial site?

(50) Which presidential library opened in Simi Valley, California in 1991?

(51) Established by Judith Ellen Foster, the Woman's National Republican Association was the first woman's partisan organization formally recognized by the Republican Party. In which year was this organization established? (a) 1888, (b) 1901, (c) 1929, (d) 1952

(52) In 1947, the Boulder Dam in Nevada was officially renamed by Congress to honor a former Republican president. What new name was the dam given?

11/6/1860 ► **Abraham Lincoln is elected president, winning only 39% of the popular vote.**

(53) Which color is most associated with the Republican Party?

(54) In front of which hotel in Washington, D.C. did the assassination attempt of Ronald Reagan occur?

(55) Scheduled for commission in mid-2009, the tenth and last Nimitz-class supercarrier of the United States Navy is named for a Republican president. For whom is this ship so named?

(56) Opposition to the 1854 Kansas-Nebraska Act was the spark that created the Republican Party. What did this act authorize?

(57) If you want to visit the Lincoln Boyhood National Memorial, to which state would you go?

(58) What does G.O.P. stand for?

(59) Held annually in February or March, this celebration is the primary annual fundraising event of many state and county organizations of the Republican Party. Name this celebration.

(60) Founded in 1892, this organization of college and university students is active in its support of the Republican Party. Name this Washington-based organization presently chaired by Charlie Smith.

(61) In which town in Illinois can you find a home of Ulysses S. Grant?

(62) What is the official color of the Republican Party?

(63) A design motif of the Lincoln Memorial can be found on the back of which U.S. dollar bill?

(64) Theodore Roosevelt was responsible for building the Sagamore Hill estate. Where can you find this estate?

(65) This memorial wall, containing the names of approximately 58,000 fallen American military men and women, was completed in 1982 in Washington, D.C. during the presidency of Ronald Reagan. Name this famous wall.

(66) Which organization did Jerry Falwell of Virginia establish in 1979?

(67) Early in its history and in response to the events of the day, the Republican Party changed its name for one election. What name did the Republican Party select?

(68) About how many Americans are registered members of the Republican Party? (a) 17 million, (b) 28 million, (c) 42 million, (d) 55 million

(69) Although considered an urban legend by the National Park Service, whose face is carved onto the back of Abraham Lincoln's statue in the Lincoln Memorial?

(70) This island, formerly known as My Lord's Island, is an 88-acre nature area situated in the middle of the Potomac River in Washington, DC. Name this island.

(71) In front of which memorial to a Republican president did Martin Luther King deliver his famous "I Have a Dream" speech in 1963?

(72) What classic symbol of the Republican Party was made famous by a cartoon by Thomas Nast published in *Harper's Weekly* on November 7, 1874?

(73) Located in Freemont, Ohio, the home of this former president has gates that were used at the White House during his presidency. Name this Republican president.

(74) Of the first ten Republican presidents, seven were born in the same state. Name this state.

(75) Many people consider Jackson, Michigan to be the birthplace of the Republican Party. What other city makes this claim?

(76) Only one state capital is named in honor of a Republican president. Name this capital.

CHAPTER
T·W·O

ACHIEVEMENTS & FIRSTS

Contributions Republicans Have Given America

"*Prosperity cannot be restored by raids upon the public treasury.***"**

- HERBERT HOOVER

"*A man is not finished when he's defeated; he's finished
when he quits.***"**

- RICHARD NIXON

(77) Only one American has held the highest position in both the executive branch of government (president) and the judicial branch of government (Supreme Court chief justice). Name this Republican.

(78) At the urging of Theodore Roosevelt, the face of which president was the first to appear on a U.S. coin? (Hint: 1909)

(79) Which Republican was the first Eagle Scout to become president?

(80) Which Republican was the first to be president of all fifty states?

(81) During which election did the Republican Party add 117 seats in the House of Representatives, marking the great transfer of strength from one party to another in United States history? (a) 1868, (b) 1876, (c) 1894, (d) 1908, (e) 1920

(82) Which Republican was named *TIME* magazine's "Man of the Year" in 1995?

(83) Which former Republican congressman and Californian won two gold Olympic medals in the decathlon?

(84) Under the leadership of Theodore Roosevelt, which U.S. naval flotilla consisting of 16 battleships was put to sea and completed a circumnavigation of the globe from December 1907 to February 1909 to demonstrate America's emergence as a world power?

(85) Who is the only American president to have parachuted—once in 1944 and again in 1997?

(86) Which Republican was the first American president to be filmed?

(87) Which Republican was the first American president to wear contact lenses?

(88) Which president and Quaker boasted reading the entire Bible by the age of ten?

(89) What distinction do Republicans Clara Cressingham, Carrie C. Holly, and Frances S. Klock of Colorado hold?

(90) Which president was the first to receive a pilot's license and first to usher in the use of helicopters for official presidential business?

(91) Born in Havana, Cuba in 1952, this Republican is the first Hispanic-American woman in the U.S. House of Representatives (1989-present) and the first Cuban American elected to Congress. Name her.

(92) Which first lady was the first to earn a college degree?

(93) In 1910, this former president flew for four minutes in an airplane made by the Wright brothers thus making him the first president to fly. Name him.

(94) Before women's right to vote was ratified on the federal level, how many individual states already extended such a right to women on the state level?

(95) Which American president and his wife were the first to place a Christmas tree in the White House?

> **IT HAPPENED ON FEBRUARY 1, 1992**
>
> ► President George H. W. Bush and Boris Yeltsin, newly elected president of Russia, meet at Camp David. Both men formally declare the end of the Cold War.

(96) In 1944, General Dwight D. Eisenhower organized the largest seaborne invasion in world history. What was this "operation" named? (Hint: Not D-Day)

5/20/1862 ▶ Republicans pass the Homestead Act of 1862 to promote individual ownership of land.

(97) Who is the only incumbent Republican president to seek another term in office, but fail to receive the party's nomination?

(98) Which future Republican president modeled for *Look* magazine in 1940 and was on the cover of *Cosmopolitan* magazine in 1942?

(99) Which government agency—charged with oversight of government expenditures—did Warren Harding and the Republican Congress create in 1921?

(100) The Foraker Act was passed under the leadership of William McKinley. What did this act establish for Puerto Rico?

REPUBLICAN TOP 10
Oldest Presidents at Inauguration

	PRESIDENT	AGE
1	Ronald Reagan	69
2	George H. W. Bush	64
3	Dwight D. Eisenhower	62
4	Gerald Ford	61
5	Richard Nixon	56
6	Warren Harding	55
7	Benjamin Harrison	55
8	George W. Bush	54
9	Herbert Hoover	54
10	William McKinley	54

(101) President George W. Bush was twice named *TIME* magazine's "Person of the Year." Which two years did he receive this recognition?

(102) In 1978, this Republican from Kansas became the first woman elected to the U.S. Senate without first having been preceded by her husband in Congress or first being appointed to fill an unexpired term. Name this Republican who also became the first woman to chair a Senate committee.

(103) Under the leadership of which Republican president was the Department of Agriculture established?

(104) The Interstate Highway System (popularly known as the National Interstate and Defense Highways Act), calling for 41,000 miles of new freeways, was championed by which Republican president?

7/2/1862 ▶ **Republicans pass the Morrill Land-Grant College Act to provide federal land grants to state colleges.**

(105) In 1929, Frank Kellogg, Secretary of State for Calvin Coolidge, won a notable international prize for his role in negotiating the Kellogg-Brand Pact. Which prize was he awarded?

(106) During the presidency of Herbert Hoover and under the direction of Senator Arthur Vandenberg of Michigan, which entity was created by the 1933 Glass-Steagall Act that today insures deposits held at financial and banking institutions?

(107) In 1964, this Republican and senator from Maine became the first woman of either major party to be nominated for president. Name this Republican who also became the first woman elected to serve in both the House and Senate.

(108) What distinction does Republican Octaviano Larrazolo of New Mexico hold?

(109) In 1937, this Republican became the first woman to hold the title of assistant chairman of the Republican National Committee and, in 1938, founded the National Federation of Republican Women. Name her.

(110) Which Republican president was most responsible for bringing an end to the Korean War?

(111) Which Republican was named "Man of the Year" by *TIME* magazine in 1990?

(112) As a New York lawyer, this future president handled a case in which blacks won the right to ride in the same street cars as whites. Name this Republican.

(113) The tradition of American presidents planting commemorative trees started with which Republican?

(114) This Republican was not only awarded the Nobel Peace Prize for helping to negotiate an end to the Russo-Japanese War, but also the first American to win the award. Name him.

1/1/1863 ▶ Abraham Lincoln issues the Emancipation Proclamation, freeing slaves in most of the Confederacy.

(115) Which Republican was the first president to nominate a woman to the United States Supreme Court?

(116) In 1989, George H. W. Bush added which post to his presidential cabinet and appointed Edward Derwinski its first secretary?

(117) Who was appointed the very first supreme commander of NATO in 1951?

(118) Which Republican president, in cooperation with Canada, oversaw the opening of the St. Lawrence Seaway?

(119) Which Republican president held the first televised press conference and was the first to use cosmetics to enhance his appearance?

(120) This wife of an early president was referred to as the "First Lady of the Land," a title later shortened to the now common usage "First Lady." Name this person.

(121) The "Star-Spangled Banner" became the national anthem during the presidency of which Republican?

(122) In 2007, this Republican was elected governor of Louisiana at age 36 making him the youngest current governor in the United States, the first non-white governor of Louisiana since Reconstruction, and the first elected Indian-American governor. Name him.

(123) In addition to three Air Medals, which individual medal did George H. W. Bush receive for his actions as a naval aviator in World War II?

(124) Which Republican president signed into law the Americans with Disabilities Act and Clean Air Act?

3/3/1863 ▶ Abraham Lincoln approves the creation of the National Academy of Sciences.

(125) Only one American president received a patent for an invention. Name the president who received a patent for a device intended to lift boats over shoals.

(126) Which Republican started the tradition of the American president tossing out the first ball at the opening of the baseball season?

(127) The 25th Amendment to the United States Constitution allows the president to nominate a new vice president, subject to congressional approval. Who was the first person nominated for vice president under this amendment?

(128) Only two children of American presidents, both Republican, have received the Congressional Medal of Honor for their heroic military service. Name the two children.

IT HAPPENED ON JUNE 28, 1902

▶ The Republican-controlled Congress passes the Spooner Act, which authorizes the funding and constructing of a canal across the Isthmus of Panama, then a province of Columbia. Also authorized in the act is a canal through Nicaragua if the canal through the isthmus is unsuccessful.

(129) Which president is associated with the Emancipation Proclamation?

(130) In 1894, this Republican became the first woman elected to state office upon becoming the superintendent of public instruction for the state of Wyoming. Name her.

(131) This president appointed the first female National Security Advisor, first female Secretary of the Interior, and first female Secretary of Agriculture. Name him.

(132) This Republican was named "Man of the Year" by *TIME* magazine in 1944 and 1959. Name him.

(133) After the outbreak of World War I, this future Republican president helped provide food and clothing to millions in Belgium and Russia left destitute by fighting. Name him.

(134) What honor was bestowed upon Rudolph Giuliani by Queen Elizabeth II for his leadership in the aftermath of the 2001 terrorist attack?

(135) Which amendment to the United States Constitution—introduced by Republicans, passed by a Republican-controlled congress, and ratified by Republican-controlled state legislatures—gave women the right to vote?

(136) The President's Council on Youth Fitness was established to encourage American children to be healthy and active children. Which president established this program?

(137) This president, the first to graduate from law school, was in office when the first telephone was installed in the White House. Name him.

(138) Prior to becoming president, which Republican became a self-made millionaire as a mining engineer on five continents?

(139) In 1880, President Rutherford B. Hayes visited San Francisco. What milestone did this visit usher in?

(140) Who is the longest living Republican president to date?

(141) This Republican president established the National Forest Service in the Department of Agriculture. Name him.

(142) This Californian was the first ever Hispanic American to serve in the U.S. House of Representatives. Name this Republican who joined Congress in 1877.

(143) Only one American president has been honored by having his likeness placed on a U.S. coin while he was still living. Name the Republican president.

(144) Prior to its current name, the White House was often referred to as the President's House or the Executive Mansion. Which Republican first used the name White House?

11/8/1864 ► **President Lincoln is reelected to a second term in office having won all states except Kentucky, New Jersey, and Delaware.**

(145) Only one Republican president did not attend college. Name him.

(146) Which person was the youngest of all Republican vice presidents upon inauguration?

(147) Which Republican was the youngest ever Chief of Staff in a presidential election?

(148) Which Republican achieved the greatest percentage point presidential election margin of victory (60.3% to 34.1%) in the popular vote?

(149) This Republican from Montana was the first woman ever elected to U.S. Congress having served from 1917 to 1919 and again from 1941 to 1942. Name her.

(150) The United States Forest Service was established by the Forest Reserve Act. During the presidency of which Republican was this landmark legislation passed?

(151) Which Republican was the first president to have an asteroid named for him?

William H. Taft, Warren G. Harding, and Robert Todd Lincoln, standing, left to right

(152) Jeane Kirkpatrick became the first woman U.S. representative to the United Nations. Which president appointed this Republican?

(153) Signed into law by Abraham Lincoln in 1862, this act gave title to 160 acres of undeveloped land outside of the original thirteen colonies to those who promised to develop the land. In total, this act granted title to 1.6 million homesteads accounting for 10% of all lands in the United States. Name this act.

Ultimate Republican Trivia

1/31/1865 ▶ 13th Amendment to the United States Constitution, abolishing slavery, is passed by the Republican Congress.

(154) In 1953, this Republican became the first woman U.S. ambassador to a major country when she was appointed by President Dwight D. Eisenhower to Italy. Name her.

(155) Which Republican was the very first president to visit all fifty states?

(156) Which Republican president approved the establishment of the National Academy of Sciences?

(157) Which Republican president excelled at horse riding and set a record while at West Point for jumping that stood for 25 years?

REPUBLICAN TOP 10
Youngest Presidents at Inauguration

	PRESIDENT	AGE
1	Theodore Roosevelt	42
2	Ulysses S. Grant	46
3	James Garfield	49
4	Chester Arthur	50
5	William Taft	51
6	Calvin Coolidge	51
7	Abraham Lincoln	52
8	Rutherford Hayes	54
9	William McKinley	54
10	Herbert Hoover	54

(158) Which Republican president is credited with adding the words "under God" to the Pledge of Allegiance?

(159) Which president is credited with ordering the flying of the American flag from the White House, government buildings, and other public buildings?

(160) In 1986, Kay Orr became the first Republican woman elected governor and the first woman to defeat another woman in a gubernatorial race. Which state did she serve?

(161) George Washington and Thomas Jefferson are two of the four presidents honored at Mt. Rushmore. Name the other two presidents, both Republicans.

(162) Born in St. Louis, Missouri in 1953, this Republican is the first female governor of Hawaii as well as the first Jewish governor of Hawaii. Name her.

4/14/1865 ▶ **President Abraham Lincoln is shot by John Wilkes Booth at Ford's theater and dies the next morning.**

(163) Which president was the first to have electricity installed in the White House?

(164) Elected in 2004, this Cuban-born Republican is the first Cuban American to serve in the United States Senate. Name this former Secretary of Housing and Urban Development under President George W. Bush.

(165) During the presidency of this Republican, a record six states were admitted to the Union. Name this president who approved statehood for North Dakota, South Dakota, Montana, Washington, Idaho, and Wyoming.

(166) Which Republican mayor was named *TIME* magazine's "Person of the Year" in the early 2000s?

(167) Which U.S. Secretary of State, along with Le Duc Tho of North Vietnam, won the Nobel Peace Prize in 1973 for their efforts in negotiating the Paris Peace Accords?

(168) Which president coined the term "normalcy" and thereby passed the word into common usage today?

(169) Which Republican and former sportscaster hosts the number one nationally syndicated radio talk show in the United States?

(170) In 1933, Republican Minnie Davenport Craig became the first woman elected to be Speaker of the House in a state legislature. Which state did she serve?

(171) Appointed Secretary of Labor by President George W. Bush in 2001, this woman became the first Asian-American woman to serve in a presidential cabinet. Name her.

(172) In 1924, this city council president became acting mayor of Seattle and elected mayor in her own right two years later. Name this Republican considered the first woman to lead a major American city.

(173) This Republican president holds the record (56 times) for the most appearances on the front cover of *TIME* magazine since its launch in 1923. Name this Republican.

(174) Which American president is recognized as the first golfing president?

(175) This future Republican president was the youngest member of Stanford University's first graduating class. Name him.

(176) Ulysses S. Grant was the second person in U.S. history to attain what military rank?

(177) Which Republican president was the first to ride in an automobile?

IT HAPPENED ON OCTOBER 17, 1973

▶ To protest American support for Israel during the Yom Kippur War, Arab countries institute an oil embargo against the United States. On March 17, 1974, Arab oil ministers, with the exception of Libya, announce the end of the embargo against the United States.

(178) In 1878, Republican President Rutherford B. Hayes made the first telephone call from the White House. Who did Hayes call?

(179) What distinction does Joseph Rainey, a former Republican congressman from South Carolina, hold?

(180) This former U.S. attorney turned Republican mayor is credited with garnering over 4,000 convictions—including insider traders Ivan Boesky and Michael Milken—and broke up the Gambino crime family control of waste disposal. Name him.

(181) Which islands were formally annexed by the United States through peaceful measures under the presidency of William McKinley?

(182) Lauro Cavazos, former Secretary of Education, was the first Hispanic American to serve in a presidential cabinet. Name the Republican president who appointed him.

(183) In 1986, this Republican became the first woman and the first Republican elected to the U.S. House of Representatives from Hawaii and became the first Asian-American woman elected to U.S. Congress. Name her.

(184) Under the leadership of which Republican president was the Americans with Disabilities Act established?

(185) Which Republican president started the Easter egg roll on the White House lawn, a tradition celebrated by each subsequent American president?

(186) This Republican was the first American of African ancestry (biracial) governor of a U.S. state, an accomplishment that was not repeated until 1990. Name this former and short-term governor of Louisiana.

(187) During the presidency of Dwight Eisenhower, the first American satellite was launched from Cape Canaveral, Florida. Name this satellite launched in 1958.

(188) Republican President Ulysses S. Grant is credited with establishing the first national park in the United States. Name this park.

(189) Which Republican won the greatest number of electoral votes by a single presidential candidate in election history?

(190) Authorized by the Pacific Railway Act, the First Transcontinental Railroad, linking the Eastern United States with California, was one of the crowning achievements of which American president?

(191) Oscar S. Straus became the first Jewish presidential cabinet member as Secretary of Commerce and Labor. Which Republican appointed him?

(192) Which important national holiday was established by President Abraham Lincoln?

(193) Under the leadership of Calvin Coolidge, the Snyder Act of 1924 was passed thereby granting citizenship to what group of people?

(194) At a height of approximately 20,320 feet, this mountain in Alaska is the highest peak in North America. After which Republican president is this mountain so named?

(195) Which Republican president helped establish UNICEF (United Nations Children's Fund), an international organization fighting for children's rights?

(196) The 15th Amendment to the United States Constitution was passed during the presidency of Ulysses S. Grant. For what did the 15th Amendment provide?

(197) Which Republican was the only preacher to become president? (Hint: Disciples of Christ)

(198) In 1955, this Republican and former speaker of the Vermont House of Representatives became the first woman ever elected lieutenant governor of a state, a role that made her president of the state Senate.

Name this Republican who thus became the only woman ever to preside over both chambers of a state legislature.

(199) Which airport in New York is named for the first New York City mayor of Italian ancestry and a sometime Republican?

(200) Which president established the Environmental Protection Agency (EPA) and approved the Clean Air Act?

(201) How many times was Ronald Reagan named "Man of the Year" by *TIME* magazine?

11/3/1868 ▶ **Ulysses S. Grant is elected president by 300,000 votes after winning roughly 450,000 African-American votes.**

(202) Who was the only president born on the 4th of July, Independence Day?

(203) Which major trade agreement, creating the world's biggest free trade zone, did President George H. W. Bush sign in 1992?

(204) Which president was the first to be born outside of the thirteen original states?

(205) Although John F. Kennedy was the youngest president-elect, he was not the youngest president in history. Name the Republican who holds this honor.

(206) In 1988, this Republican from New Mexico became the first female veteran and the first Air Force Academy graduate elected to the U.S. House of Representatives. Name her.

(207) Under the leadership of which president was the Hay-Pauncefort Treaty signed granting the United States permission to build and operate the Panama Canal?

(208) Which Republican was the first president of the United States to be born west of the Mississippi River?

(209) Dr. Antonia C. Novello, the first woman and first Hispanic-American surgeon general, was appointed by which Republican president?

(210) What did President Theodore Roosevelt establish on Pelican Island, Florida in 1903?

(211) On January 16, 2001, this Republican became the first president to receive (posthumously) the Medal of Honor, the highest award for military service given in the United States. Name him.

(212) In late 1943, what distinction did George H. W. Bush earn when, at age 19, he was commissioned an ensign in the U.S. Navy?

(213) Which Republican was named *TIME* magazine's "Man of the Year" in 1971 and 1972?

(214) In 1906, President Theodore Roosevelt signed an act that established 18 national monuments, including Devils Tower, Muir Woods, and Mount Olympus. Which act did he sign?

(215) In 1965, this tank driver snuck off an Austrian army base to compete and subsequently win his first bodybuilding competition, Mr. Junior Europe. Name this Republican.

(216) Which Republican was the only president to serve in both World Wars?

(217) The Portsmouth Peace Conference held in Portsmouth, New Hampshire was held during the presidency of Theodore Roosevelt. What did this conference establish?

(218) This Republican from the state of Hawaii was the first person of Chinese-American ancestry elected to the U.S. Senate. Name this man who served from 1959 to 1976.

(219) Which Republican president created the double-billed cabinet post, divided into two cabinet posts in 1913, of Secretary of Commerce and Labor?

(220) Which Republican president was awarded the Presidential Medal of Freedom, the nation's highest civilian honor, in 1999?

CHAPTER III
T·H·R·E·E

OFFICE OF THE PRESIDENT

Inside the Oval Office

"He serves his party best who serves the country best."

- RUTHERFORD B. HAYES

"Government can and must provide opportunity, not smother it; foster productivity, not stifle it."

- RONALD REAGAN

Ultimate Republican Trivia

2/3/1870 ► Republican dominated governments ratify the 15th Amendment granting African-American men the right to vote.

(221) Prior to the death of Abraham Lincoln, how many American presidents were assassinated?

(222) During the presidency of which Republican was the 26th Amendment, reducing the voting age from 21 to 18, to the United States Constitution passed?

(223) Which two states, one a "breakaway" state, were admitted to the Union during the Civil War when Abraham Lincoln was president?

(224) Only one Confederate state was completely exempt from Abraham Lincoln's Emancipation Proclamation. Name the state.

(225) This scholarly Republican president could read and write German, Latin, and Greek. Name him.

(226) Which three Republican presidents never were elected to public office prior to becoming president?

(227) When this president and his wife did not want others to know what they were speaking, the two would often speak in Chinese. Name the president.

(228) Which Republican president installed a mechanical horse at the White House as a way to supplant his passion for horseback riding?

(229) Who replaced the name "chairman" with the now commonly used name "administrator" for heads of government agencies and committees?

(230) Which Republican president said about the White House, "You don't live there. You are only Exhibit A to the country"?

(231) "I think he has hardly a friend left, except myself" was uttered by Abraham Lincoln in reference to which American leader willing to accept heavy casualties in order to win battles?

(232) Which Republican president served during the years 1901 to 1909?

(233) This Republican president participated in twice-weekly poker games in a group he dubbed the "Poker Cabinet." Name him.

(234) Which church/religious affiliation did Dwight Eisenhower join the day after being elected president?

(235) Ronald Reagan served two terms as governor of which state?

(236) Which early Republican president is known for the nickname "Railsplitter," a name bestowed by the Illinois State Republican Convention?

(237) This Republican president replaced a portrait of Harry S. Truman with a portrait of Calvin Coolidge in the White House Cabinet room to show his support of Coolidge's limited government philosophy. Name him.

(238) Which Republican president did Ronald Reagan often cite as a mentor because of his tax cuts on four occasions?

(239) In 1956, President Dwight D. Eisenhower condemned Britain, France, and Israel for their combined attack on which nation?

(240) While hunting near Yazoo City, Mississippi in 1902, this Republican refused to shoot a bear cub. Thereafter his first name became synonymous with a popular stuffed animal. Name this Republican.

(241) In January 1961, President Dwight D. Eisenhower severed diplomatic relations with which leftist island country?

(242) "Speak softly and carry a big stick" is an expression coined by which Republican president?

(243) Of the 18 Republican presidents, how many completed two full terms in the White House?

(244) The Reagan administration provided military assistance and economic aid to rebels fighting the Sandinistas in which Central American country?

(245) In 1971, Richard Nixon commuted the prison sentence of what noted labor leader?

(246) Which Republican and noted man of few words said, "If you don't say anything, you won't be called on to repeat it"?

(247) This president is remembered for his speech beginning with "Four score and seven years ago." Name this Republican.

(248) Herbert Hoover was given a one-syllable nickname by his close friends. What was this nickname?

(249) Which Republican advanced the party doctrine termed "Modern Republicanism"?

(250) Which world leader did Theodore Roosevelt dislike because he would not stand when ladies entered the room?

(251) Under which Republican president was the first cabinet meeting televised?

(252) This territory, formally known as the Indian Territory, was formally admitted as a state during the presidency of Theodore Roosevelt. Name this state.

(253) Following the Watergate scandal, which president gave Richard Nixon a "full, free, and absolute pardon"?

(254) In 1972, Richard Nixon signed the historic SALT (Strategic Arms Limitation Talks) Agreement to curb nuclear proliferation. With which Soviet leader did he sign the agreement?

3/10/1872 ▶ President Grant establishes a special commission to select the best canal route across Central America—ultimately selecting Nicaragua.

(255) Name the future Republican president who worked on military training films during World War II.

(256) Which Republican was known for reading through three major newspapers by 7:30am each morning?

(257) This Republican was the only president to be wounded and survive an assassination attempt. Name him.

(258) Who was Dwight D. Eisenhower's vice president?

(259) Prior to John McCain and the 2008 presidential election, who was the oldest elected president in American history?

(260) Gerald Ford assumed the role of president upon the resignation of Richard Nixon. Who did Ford nominate to become his vice president?

(261) "Government always finds a need for whatever money it gets" was said by which Republican president?

(262) Which letter of the alphabet was missing—perpetrated by the Clinton staff prior to leaving—from most of the keyboards in the White House when George W. Bush took office?

(263) Although Warren Harding golfed twice each week while president, what was his preferred extracurricular activity? (Hint: Gambling)

(264) This president de-manded that all furniture in the White House be auctioned off and replaced with new furniture before he moved in. Name him.

IT HAPPENED ON OCTOBER 25, 1983

▶ In response to the assassination of Prime Minister Maurice Bishop in a military coup, President Ronald Reagan dispatches American forces to Grenada to protect nearly 1,000 American students on the island. American forces quickly defeat the initial resistance of over 700 Cuban soldiers and restore order.

(265) Weighing over 330 pounds and nicknamed "Big Lub," this Republican president once got himself stuck in the White House bath tub. As a result, he had a new bath tub installed, big enough to hold four people. Name him.

(266) Which Republican president encouraged Americans to be "Citizens, not spectators" and "Citizens, not subjects"?

(267) This president was so tone deaf that he had to be nudged when to stand up for the playing of the national anthem. Name this Republican.

(268) Who became the first president to resign from office?

(269) What unique writing skill did Republican President James Garfield boast?

(270) This American president was known for his constant doodling at work. Name this Republican.

(271) Which Republican president hated music since it made him feel ill?

(272) Ronald Reagan ordered air strikes against Libya for its role in sponsoring terrorist activities. Which Libyan leader masterminded the activities?

(273) What is unusual about the years in which Republican presidents Lincoln, Garfield, McKinley, and Reagan were shot and all but Reagan assassinated?

(274) This president removed the White House greenhouse and erected the office suite now known as the West Wing. Name the president.

(275) In 1869, the Grant administration attempted to annex a certain Caribbean island country only to see the Senate reject the plan the following summer. Name this present-day country.

(276) Which doctrine, named for a Republican president, pledged aid to any Middle Eastern country combating Communism?

3/4/1873 ▶ President Grant is reelected to a second term in office.

(277) Which Republican was the first American president to visit China and the Soviet Union while in office?

(278) The bust of which president was placed in the Oval Office by President Gerald Ford?

(279) Except for his formal signature, how did Gerald Ford sign his name?

(280) This president and devout Presbyterian prohibited conducting state business on Sundays. Name this Republican.

(281) Which Republican president described himself as a "compassionate conservative"?

(282) Who is the first United States Military Academy graduate to become President of the United States?

(283) Who was the only president to visit the floor of the New York Stock Exchange while in office?

(284) This Republican president advanced "the Square Deal" platform by enforcing anti-trust laws to preserve a balance among competing economic interests. Name him.

(285) Republican President Dwight D. Eisenhower signed two statehood bills during his time in office. Name the two states.

(286) This plan, an important initiative of Ronald Reagan in the 1980 presidential election, was to rebuild the United States Navy after cutbacks that followed the end of the Vietnam War. The plan included recommissioning Iowa-class battleships, keeping older ships in service, and building new ships. What was the name for this plan?

(287) Which Republican president and former military man suffered a heart attack and had an intestinal bypass operation while in office?

(288) Which two Republican presidents never gave inaugural addresses?

(289) Which president had vice presidents Garrett Hobart and Theodore Roosevelt in his first and second terms in office, respectively?

(290) Which Republican president instituted economic sanctions against South Africa as a result of its apartheid policies?

(291) The daughter of this president claimed her father was "the bride at every wedding, the corpse at every funeral." Name the president.

(292) In his first two years in office, this president appointed more women to serve in top policy-making positions than any other president for a comparable period of time. Name him.

(293) This president and first lady, both avid bowlers, installed a one-lane bowling alley in the underground work area below the White House driveway. Name this couple.

(294) Who was the first vice president to take office through nomination by the president and confirmation by Congress rather than elected as vice president?

(295) Abraham Lincoln was the first president to be photographed at his inauguration. Surprisingly, which person can be seen standing close to Lincoln in the photo of his second inauguration?

(296) President Ronald Reagan initiated a monumental plan to cut taxes and decrease the size of the federal government. What term is often used to describe this plan?

(297) During the presidency of Dwight D. Eisenhower, a collective defense treaty was signed in 1954 in Manila, Philippines by the United States and seven other countries. Name this treaty dissolved in 1977.

11/7/1874 ▶ **The Republican elephant is created by political cartoonist Thomas Nast.**

(298) Which Republican president had the middle name Gamaliel?

(299) Who is the only Republican president not to veto Congressional legislation?

(300) Only four Republican presidents served less than one term. Name the four men.

(301) Which Republican president officially changed from horses to cars and converted the White House stables into a four-car garage?

(302) This Republican president-elect barely escaped death on the train ride to his inauguration. After the plot to kill him was uncovered, he secretly switched trains in Philadelphia for the final leg to Washington. Name him.

(303) Which Republican president coined the expression, "My hat is in the ring"?

(304) What were the names for the two major military operations (campaigns) employed during the First Gulf War? (Hint: One defensive and one offensive)

(305) Which president was known for his "Big Stick Diplomacy"?

(306) One of the notable achievements of the Ulysses S. Grant presidency was the suppression of a certain violent group. Which group did he suppress?

(307) Which Republican president presided over the dedication of the Washington Monument on February 21, 1885?

(308) Which Republican president described himself as "the First Citizen" to downplay his prominence within the American political establishment?

(309) In December 1992, President George H. W. Bush sent American troops to help in humanitarian relief efforts to which African nation torn by civil war?

(310) What financial crisis hit the country in 1989 during the presidency of George H. W. Bush?

(311) Which Republican exclaimed, "I forgot to duck"?

(312) "Forceful intervention" was demanded of Congress by Republican President William McKinley over which island nation?

(313) Which Republican president opened each cabinet meeting with silent prayer?

(314) This Republican's last words were, "I've always loved my wife. I've always loved my children. I've always loved my grandchildren. And I've always loved my country." Name him.

(315) Which Republican president frequently used "God Bless the U.S.A." from Lee Greenwood?

(316) Which American president was the first to make a radio broadcast from the White House?

(317) Three sons of this former Republican president died in combat—one in World War I and two in World War II. Name the presidential father.

(318) Which Republican president promised he would serve only one term in office—and kept his promise?

(319) This Republican president is known for his love of tennis, boxing, hunting, fishing, and martial arts. Name him.

(320) *Where's the Rest of Me?* and *An American Life* are the titles of two autobiographies from which Republican?

(321) Which president pressed into service the *Mayflower* as his presidential vessel?

(322) This Republican was often seen walking around the White House with his pet raccoon Rebecca draped around his neck. Name him.

(323) First known as Hi-Catoctin, this camp was converted to a presidential retreat in 1942 and later renamed by President Dwight D. Eisenhower after his grandson. Name this camp.

(324) Before the Emancipation Proclamation to free slaves in the Confederacy was enacted in 1863, President Abraham Lincoln signed a bill that abolished slavery in which area of the country in 1862?

(325) Abraham Lincoln was the _____ President of the United States of America? (a) 9th, (b) 16th, (c) 21st, (d) 28th

REPUBLICAN TOP 10

Presidents and Widest Margin of Election Victories

	WINNER	CHALLENGER	YEAR	MARGIN
1	Ronald Reagan	Walter Mondale	1984	97.6%
2	Richard Nixon	McGovern & Hospers	1972	96.8%
3	Abraham Lincoln	George McClellan	1864	91.0%
4	Ronald Reagan	Jimmy Carter	1990	90.9%
5	Dwight D. Eisenhower	Stevenson & Jones	1956	86.2%
6	Herbert Hoover	Al Smith	1928	83.6%
7	Dwight D. Eisenhower	Adlai Stevenson	1952	83.2%
8	Ulysses S. Grant	Horace Greeley	1872	81.3%
9	George H. W. Bush	Dukakis & Bentsen	1988	79.3%
10	Warren G. Harding	James Middleton Cox	1920	76.1%

Note: Ranked by Percentage of Available Electoral Votes Won

(326) This president had a habit of changing his clothes multiple times each day. Name this "elegant" Republican.

(327) Ronald Reagan's economic plan called for substantial tax cuts that, in time, would generate higher government revenue as a result of the increased economic output from lower taxes. What was the name for this plan?

(328) Admitted in 1912 during the presidency of Republican William H. Taft, these two states created the forty-eight contiguous states as we know it today. Name these two states.

(329) Which Republican president and devout Methodist invited guests to the White House Blue Room to "hymn sings"?

(330) To whom did President Richard Nixon submit his letter of resignation?

(331) *Crowded Hours* was a "tell all" book about the extraordinary and wild behavior taking place in the White House during the Harding administration. Who wrote this book published in 1933?

(332) Even though he learned to tolerate it, what nickname did Abraham Lincoln hate to be called?

(333) Where did President Abraham Lincoln typically carry important government documents?

(334) The Gettysburg Address is arguably one of the most important speeches of any American president. How long was this speech by Abraham Lincoln?

(335) Which Republican president told Soviet leader Mikhail Gorbachev to "tear down this wall (Berlin Wall)"?

(336) Which Republican president reversed his first and middle names to avoid confusion with his father of the same name?

(337) The 20th Amendment to the United States Constitution moved the inauguration of the president and date for Congress to convene from March to January. Under the leadership of which president was this amendment ratified?

(338) This state, nicknamed the Centennial State, was admitted to the Union in 1876 during the presidency of Ulysses S. Grant. Name this state.

(339) This Republican president was neither elected president nor elected vice president. Name him.

(340) Which Republican and future president was named governor of the Philippines by President William McKinley?

(341) In 1981, President Ronald Reagan dismissed and quickly replaced nearly 13,000 workers for violating federal law by going on strike. Who were these workers?

(342) While in office, which Republican president was arrested for riding his horse too fast through the streets of Washington, D.C., fined $20, and had his carriage impounded?

(343) "Good to the Last Drop" is a present-day marketing slogan of Maxwell House Coffee. From the quote of which Republican president did Maxwell House get this slogan?

(344) During his efforts to end the Vietnam War, which Republican president used the expression, "Peace and honor"?

(345) "America is too great for small dreams" was said by which Republican president?

(346) This Republican president rarely went to bed before 2 A.M. and was known for his strolls with guests through the streets of Washington, D.C. past midnight. Name this president.

(347) This Republican president was nicknamed Teddy, a name he hated and a name by which no one he knew well ever called him. Name this president.

(348) This Republican president so cherished the memory of his late wife that he had fresh flowers placed in front of her portrait in the White House every day. Name this president.

(349) Lynette "Squeaky" Fromme, a disciple of mass murderer Charles Manson, attempted to assassinate which president with a Colt .45 outside the Senator Hotel in San Francisco?

(350) Which American president is credited with adding the Oval Office to the White House?

(351) President Ronald Reagan pushed to develop the Strategic Defense Initiative to intercept and destroy incoming missiles. By what other name was this program referred to?

(352) In 1903, President Theodore Roosevelt signed the Hay-Bunau-Varilla Treaty whereby the United States would pay $10 million upfront and pay $250,000 annually. What did the U.S. receive in return?

Gerald R. Ford

(353) Which Republican president and avid golfer had a putting green and small sand trap installed by the U.S. Golf Association near the White House rose garden?

(354) The United States Marine Band played the song "The Lady is a Tramp" when President Gerald Ford was dancing with a popular world figure. Name her.

(355) Which president often referred to the Soviet Union as the "Evil Empire"?

(356) Which Republican is credited as the first president to use the expression, "this nation under God"?

(357) Which president is known for his expression, "Walk softly and carry a big stick"?

(358) *The Independence Review* gave Richard Nixon what nickname in 1950?

(359) Which Republican president was hearing impaired due to a gun firing near his head?

(360) In which country did future president Herbert Hoover gain wealth and fortune in silver mining as an engineer?

(361) What was Dwight Eisenhower attempting to describe when he said, "Global in scope, atheistic in character, ruthless in purpose, and insidious in method"?

(362) The year 1881 is often referred to as the "year of three presidents." Name the three Republican presidents.

(363) Which Republican was the first president to be commonly referred to by his initials?

(364) Which noted World War II radio personality was given a presidential pardon by Gerald Ford?

(365) Which currency was Abraham Lincoln carrying in his pocket on the night he was shot at Ford's Theater?

(366) In 1957, Dwight D. Eisenhower pushed for more spending on national defense in response to what major global event?

(367) In what year did the Supreme Court order Richard Nixon to turn over to prosecutors the infamous Watergate tapes? (a) 1971, (b) 1972, (c) 1973, (d) 1974

(368) Which president had a bad habit of nodding off to sleep in public places?

(369) What rare disorder; characterized by long arms and legs, extra-long middle fingers, and a sunken chest; do some medical experts claim inflicted Abraham Lincoln?

(370) "A madman, an imbecile, and a bum" were the words spoken by which foreign leader in reference to Ronald Reagan?

(371) What was the code name for the 2003 military air campaign against Bagdad while U.S. ground troops secured the southern region of Iraq?

(372) Which Republican president was known for his excessive sleeping of nearly eleven hours each day?

(373) Which Republican president offered a pardon to thousands of Vietnam War draft dodgers and military deserters if they commit— although few did—to two years of public service?

(374) Which Republican president had twelve vetoes overridden by Congress, the most of any Republican?

(375) Of the 181 vetoes by President Dwight D. Eisenhower, how many were overridden by Congress?

(376) Which disease led to the decline and ultimate death of Ronald Reagan?

(377) Which cabinet post was removed, or "de-Cabinetized," by Richard Nixon in 1969 and transformed into a self-supporting corporation wholly owned by the federal government?

(378) "Silent Cal" was the nickname given to which Republican president?

(379) George W. Bush ranks as the 43rd President of the United States. What sequence of vice presidents does Richard "Dick" Chaney rank?

(380) Which European nation did President William McKinley ask Congress to declare war on in April 1898?

(381) The United States nearly went to war with a South American country during the presidency of Benjamin Harrison over the killing of two sailors while on shore leave from the U.S.S. *Baltimore*. Name this country.

4/24/1877 ▶ **Federal troops are withdrawn from Louisiana by President Hayes effectively ending Reconstruction.**

(382) This Republican became the first American president to journey overseas when he and his wife traveled to Panama. Name him.

(383) This Republican president wrote *Real Peace*, *The Real War*, and *No More Vietnams*. Name him.

(384) Which Republican president did Lynette Fromme and Sara Jane Moore attempt to assassinate on separate occasions within a 17-day period only to fail and receive life sentences?

(385) Which president established the interdenominational White House prayer breakfasts?

(386) What was Ronald Reagan referring to when he said, "We built it, we paid for it, it's ours, and we're going to keep it"?

(387) In 1989, President George H. W. Bush sent American troops into Panama to capture which drug-trafficking military dictator?

(388) What caused President Gerald Ford's approval rating to decline from 71% to 50% in one week?

IT HAPPENED ON MARCH 16, 1882

▶ The Geneva Convention of 1864, also known as the Red Cross Treaty, is ratified by the U.S. Senate two weeks after President Chester Arthur declared his support for the measure. This treaty stipulates that hospitals, ambulances, medical staff, and chaplains are to be considered neutral parties.

(389) Who came up with the eleventh commandment: "Thou shalt not speak ill of another Republican"?

(390) What type of people was Ronald Reagan referring to when he said, "(They) act like Tarzan, look like Jane, and smell like Cheetah"?

(391) Which future Republican president earned $500,000 in royalties for his book titled *Crusade in Europe* he wrote about his military experiences before becoming president?

(392) Which four Republican vice presidents were elevated to president in mid-term?

Ultimate Republican Trivia

3/1/1878 ▶ President Hayes vetoes a bill that bans immigration from China.

(393) This Republican president hung big-game hunting trophies in the State Dining Room. Name him.

(394) Which Republican president held office during the Wall Street crash of 1929?

(395) When the "Bonus Expeditionary Force," a group of World War I veterans and their families, marched on Washington demanding service bonuses, which military man did President Herbert Hoover instruct to deal with the crowd?

(396) In 1993, President George H. W. Bush and Russian President Boris Yeltsin signed a historic agreement providing for the reduction of nuclear arsenals to about one-third of their present levels within ten years. Name this agreement.

(397) Which Republican president was such an avid reader that he read two to three books on average per day while in office?

(398) "Axis of Evil" was an expression used by President George W. Bush in his State of the Union Address on January 29, 2002. Which three countries comprised this axis?

(399) President Gerald Ford signed legislation to bail out which financially troubled American city in 1975?

(400) This Republican president exclaimed, "I can be President of the United States, or I can control Alice (his daughter). I can't possibly do both." Name him.

(401) Which president was sometimes referred to as the "human iceberg" for his stiff and formal demeanor?

CHAPTER F·O·U·R
IV

CONGRESS, CABINETS, & COURTS

Trailblazing Republican Leaders

"My failures have been errors of judgment, not of intent."

- ULYSSES S. GRANT

"Next to the right of liberty, the right of property is the most important individual right guaranteed by the Constitution...."

- WILLIAM HOWARD TAFT

43

(402) Who was appointed head of the Federal Bureau of Investigation by Harlan Stone, a Calvin Coolidge cabinet member?

(403) Republican Senator Robert A. Taft, son of former president William H. Taft, was commonly referred to by what nickname?

(404) Born on May 7, 1932 in Albuquerque, New Mexico, this senator is one of five children of Italian immigrants from Lucca, Tuscany. He is also the first Republican in 38 years elected from New Mexico to the United States Senate. Name this senator who announced that he will not run for re-election in 2008.

(405) Which Republican in the Ford administration resigned in protest over President Ford's pardoning of Richard Nixon?

(406) This future Republican president served as Secretary of Commerce for both Warren G. Harding and Calvin Coolidge. Name him.

(407) Henry Kissinger, Secretary of State for President Richard Nixon, wrote a book about foreign affairs in the Nixon administration. Name the title of this book.

(408) This Reagan cabinet member attempted, but failed, to negotiate a settlement over the Falkland Islands between Britain and Argentina. Name him.

(409) Who was President Ford's lone nominee to the United States Supreme Court?

(410) Which two African Americans held the post of Security of State under President George W. Bush?

(411) Born in 1952 in East Lansing, Michigan, this Republican is a former United States senator from Michigan and the 10th United States Secretary of Energy, serving under President George W. Bush. Name this person.

(412) Which early Republican was nicknamed the "Plumed Knight"?

7/2/1881 ▶ President James A. Garfield is shot by Charles Guiteau, a Washington lawyer.

(413) This Republican, the first African-American Secretary of State (2001-2005), served as National Security Advisor (1987–1989), and as Chairman of the Joint Chiefs of Staff (1989–1993). Name this patriotic American.

(414) Which Republican president fixed the number of Supreme Court justices at nine, the present number today?

(415) Name the two Supreme Court nominees of President George H. W. Bush confirmed by the Senate.

(416) This Republican, a former five-term U.S. senator and former chairman of the Senate Foreign Relations Committee, remains the longest-serving popularly-elected U.S. senator in North Carolina history. Name this Republican whose Senate seat was won by Elizabeth Dole when he retired in 2002.

(417) This South Carolina senator, formally a colonel in the United States Air Force, serves on the Armed Services and Judiciary Committees and is one of the Gang of 14. Name him.

(418) The senate's Watergate committee was named for its chairman. Name this committee.

TOP 10	
Percentage of Women in State Legislatures	

	STATE	%
1	Vermont	37.8
2	New Hampshire	35.8
3	Washington	35.4
4	Colorado	35.0
5	Minnesota	34.8
6	Hawaii	32.9
7	Arizona	32.2
8	Maryland	31.4
9	Maine	31.2
10	Oregon	31.1

Source: National Federation of Republican Women, 2008

(419) Which controversial anti-terrorism bill authorizing law enforcement and intelligence agencies to investigate terrorist suspects and carry out wiretapping and surveillance did President George W. Bush sign on October 26, 2001?

(420) Who was nominated by Ronald Reagan to the Supreme Court but rejected by the Senate for being overly conservative?

(421) According to the Congressional Biographical Directory, what is the first and middle names of J. C. Watts, former congressman from Oklahoma?

(422) Signed into law in 2002, this Act seeks to improve the performance of U.S. primary and secondary schools by increasing the standards of accountability for states, school districts, and schools, as well as providing parents more flexibility in choosing which schools their children attend. Name this act.

(423) Born in 1933 in Lake Forest, Illinois, this Republican served as California state assemblyman from 1967 to 1971, as mayor of San Diego for eleven years, as U.S. senator for eight years, and became the thirty-sixth governor of California. Name this Yale graduate.

(424) Which Republican served as governor of Rhode Island, Secretary of the Navy in the Nixon administration, and became the first Republican to win a Rhode Island senate election since 1930?

(425) Which federal agency did George H. W. Bush serve as director from 1976 to 1977?

(426) Which Civil War Union general served for a brief period as Secretary of War for President Ulysses S. Grant?

(427) What son of a former president served as Secretary of War for President Chester Arthur?

(428) Casper Weinberger served as Secretary of Defense for which Republican president?

(429) This Republican, born in Bangor, Maine to a Russian-Jewish immigrant father, is a former U.S. senator and Secretary of Defense (1997–2001) under President Bill Clinton. Name him.

(430) At the suggestion of Theodore Roosevelt, which Supreme Court justice resigned from the high court and ran on the Republican ticket against Woodrow Wilson in the 1916 presidential election?

6/6/1884 ▶ **Republicans nominate James G. Blaine, leader of the Half-Breeds, for the 1884 presidential election.**

(431) Born in 1927, this Republican served as Secretary of the Navy from 1972 to 1974 and has served as U.S. senator from Virginia since 1979, but will not seek re-election in 2008. Name this Republican best known for his marriage to Elizabeth Taylor.

(432) The Consumer Product Safety Act provides for safety standards and recalls for products that present unreasonable or substantial risks of injury or death to consumers. Under which president was this act ratified by Congress.

(433) In 1965, this Republican replaced Charles Halleck to become minority leader in the U.S. House of Representatives. Name him.

(434) This attorney general for Richard Nixon served 19 months in prison for the Watergate scandal. Name him.

(435) Joseph R. McCarthy, a senator from Wisconsin, became popular for his anti-Communist stance. What label named for McCarthy became the embodiment of the growing anti-Communist spirit?

(436) This former White House counsel and lawyer was nominated by President George W. Bush on October 3, 2005 for justice of the U.S. Supreme Court to replace Justice Sandra Day O'Connor. The nomination was met with opposition from both political sides and her name was subsequently withdrawn. Name her.

(437) Prior to becoming attorney general, this Republican lost his Missouri Senate race to a dead man. Name the Republican.

3/4/1889 ▶ **Benjamin Harrison is inaugurated as the 23rd President of the United States.**

(438) This German American was a noted author, newspaper editor, Civil War Union Army general, and American statesman. In 1869, he became the first German-born American elected to the United States Senate and first German-American cabinet member. Name this Republican.

(439) This German-born American bureaucrat, diplomat, and 1973 Nobel Peace Prize laureate served as National Security Advisor and later as Secretary of State in the Richard Nixon administration. Name this Republican.

(440) This Republican is a former Buffalo Bills quarterback, long-time congressman, and Secretary of Housing and Urban Development under President George H. W. Bush. Name him.

(441) Born in 1948, this Supreme Court justice was nominated by George H. W. Bush and is considered the first conservative African American on the high court. Name him.

(442) This vice president under Richard Nixon resigned in response to charges of income tax evasion and of accepting kickbacks and bribes. Name this person who pleaded "no contest" to the charges.

(443) The Pension Act of 1880 was passed during the presidency of Benjamin Harrison. What did this act establish?

(444) Who became Speaker of the House of Representatives upon the resignation of Newt Gingrich in 1998?

(445) This associate justice of the Supreme Court was nominated by President Richard Nixon and elevated to chief justice by President Ronald Reagan after Warren Burger stepped down. Name him.

(446) Born in 1957, this CNN political contributor, author of the book *What Color is a Conservative*, and former congressman from Oklahoma is the last African-American Republican to serve in the House. Name him.

(447) Appointed U.S. attorney general in 2001 by President George W. Bush, this former senator and governor of Missouri presently serves as a Washington D.C. lobbyist. Name him.

(448) In 1998, which former U.S. senator from Tennessee provided emergency medical assistance for two gunned-down U.S. Capitol police officers and the assailant?

(449) In 1870, the Republican-controlled Congress created a department to accommodate the increasing responsibilities of the attorney general. Name this department.

(450) Who was Ronald Reagan's first nomination to the United States Supreme Court?

(451) While serving in New York state politics, this future president was known as the "Cyclone Assemblyman." Name him.

(452) Which Roman Catholic and conservative Supreme Court justice has fathered nine children and once performed with Ruth Bader Ginsberg in an opera?

(453) How many decisions did the United States Supreme Court issue to ensure the legitimacy of George W. Bush's 2000 presidential election victory?

(454) What item did Dwight F. Davis, Secretary of War under Calvin Coolidge, donate that became an international trophy? (Hint: Tennis)

(455) This justice of the Supreme Court, nominated by President Ronald Reagan, distributes short notes around the court referred to as "Ninograms." Name this person considered the most conservative voice on the Supreme Court.

(456) This former political consultant, trusted advisor to presidents Ronald Reagan and George H. W. Bush, and head of the Republican National Committee died of a brain tumor in 1991. Name this person born in Atlanta, Georgia and grew up in Aiken, South Carolina.

(457) This Republican, a former political science professor at Stanford University and White House National Security Advisor, said that her dream job would be commissioner of the National Football League. Name this woman who began playing the piano at age three.

(458) Which Republican oversaw the "strategic communications" effort of the White House Iraq Group (WHIG) regarding weapons of mass destruction in Iraq?

(459) Born in 1941, this Republican and former senator from Mississippi served in numerous leadership positions in both the House of Representatives and the Senate, including House Minority Whip, Senate Majority Leader, Senate Minority Leader, and Senate Minority Whip. Name this Republican who is the first person to have served as whip in both houses of Congress.

(460) Born in Pittsburgh, this Republican was part of the family known for their "57 Varieties." He served in the U.S. House of Representatives (1971–1977) and the United States Senate (1977–1991). Name him.

(461) Terminated by President George H. W. Bush in December 1991, this White House Chief of Staff was known for his nastiness in Washington. Name him.

(462) The Compromise of 1877 was passed during the presidency of Rutherford B. Hayes. What did this legislation stipulate?

(463) This senator from South Carolina holds the record for the longest speech in Senate history at 24 hours and 18 minutes. Who gave this very lengthy speech against the 1957 Civil Rights Act?

(464) This Princeton University educated justice of the United States Supreme Court is the grandson of Italian immigrants to America. Name this appointee of George W. Bush.

(465) Born in 1932 in Indianapolis, this man is the senior United States senator from Indiana and member of the Republican Party. He attended Oxford as a Rhodes Scholar and served in the U.S. Navy from 1957 to 1960. Name him.

(466) Which female law professor accused Clarence Thomas, a George H. W. Bush nominee to the Supreme Court, of sexual harassment?

(467) In 1884, which bureau, becoming a department in 1888, was created as a division of the Department of the Interior during the presidency of Chester Arthur?

(468) Who was President Eisenhower's nominee for chief justice to the United States Supreme Court in 1953?

(469) What cabinet post did Dick Cheney hold in the George H. W. Bush administration?

(470) This Roman Catholic and former clerk for Justice William Rehnquist is the third-youngest United States chief justice in history at age 50. Name this 2006 nominee of President George W. Bush.

(471) Born in 1930 to immigrant parents from Russia, this Republican served in the United States Air Force from 1951 to 1953, was elected U.S. senator from Pennsylvania in 1980, and is currently the 16th-most senior member of the Senate. Name this University of Pennsylvania and Yale Law School graduate.

(472) In 1974, President Ford appointed which former child movie star the ambassador to Ghana (1974-1976)?

4/19/1898 ▶ The Republican Congress authorizes President McKinley to intervene in Cuba.

(473) This Republican became the leader in the Senate after Howard Baker left politics in 1985. Name this decorated and gravely wounded World War II veteran.

(474) Which Republican is most responsible for persuading Congress to construct a separate building for the U.S. Supreme Court to meet rather than using the Capitol building?

(475) Who was the first Secretary of State for President George W. Bush?

(476) Who are the two U.S. senators, both of Italian heritage, representing the state of Wyoming in 2008?

(477) This U.S. senator, born on March 25, 1958 in Roseville, California, was named 2005 "Legislator of the Year" by the Humane Society of the United States for his commitment to the humane treatment of animals. Name this Nevada senator elected in 2000.

(478) This ten-term congressman from Georgia and Speaker of the House from 1995 to 1999 is remembered for his "Contract With America" and leading the Republican Revolution which ended 40 years of non-Republican Party rule of the House of Representatives. Name him.

(479) What did Benjamin Harrison promote in 1891 to reduce the workload of the United States Supreme Court?

(480) Which cabinet member and famous American was critically wounded by John Wilkes Booth during the assassination of Abraham Lincoln? (Hint: Purchase of Alaska)

(481) Who did Ronald Reagan appoint as Secretary of State after the resignation of Alexander Haig?

(482) Secretary of State William H. Seward agreed to purchase Alaska from Russia for $7.2 million. What did critics call this decision?

(483) Name the Secretary of Defense who, in December 2006, resigned under pressure over the handling of the Second Gulf War.

CHAPTER F·I·V·E

MOVERS, SHAKERS, & FIRST LADIES

All About Pioneering Republicans

> **"**The best minds are not in government. If any were,
> business would hire them away. **"**
>
> - RONALD REAGAN

> **"**This is not about a bigger welfare state or a cheaper welfare state. This
> is about replacing a system that is killing our children. **"**
>
> - NEWT GINGRICH

(484) *Recollections of Full Years* is a book written by which former first lady?

(485) Born in 1955, this Republican was the governor of Arkansas from 1996 to 2007 and was a Republican candidate in the 2008 United States presidential primaries. Name this person who holds the third-longest tenure of any Arkansas governor.

(486) Felix Perez Camacho, Republican governor born in 1957 in Camp Zama, Japan, is a Marquette University graduate and son of a former governor. Of which island is he governor?

(487) The China Room in the White House has a red color scheme to match the nearby portrait of a Republican first lady. Name her.

(488) This Republican became governor of Texas in December 2000 when George W. Bush resigned (to prepare for inauguration as president) and was elected to full terms in 2002 and 2006. Name this man named the 2008 chairman of the Republican Governors Association.

REPUBLICAN TOP 10
Tallest Presidents

	PRESIDENT	HEIGHT
1	Abraham Lincoln	6 ft 4 in
2	Chester A. Arthur	6 ft 2 in
3	George H. W. Bush	6 ft 2 in
4	Ronald Reagan	6 ft 2 in
t5	Gerald Ford	6 ft 0 in
t5	James Garfield	6 ft 0 in
t5	Warren Harding	6 ft 0 in
t5	William Howard Taft	6 ft 0 in
9	Richard Nixon	5 ft 11½ in
t10	George W. Bush	5 ft 11 in
t10	Herbert Hoover	5 ft 11 in

(489) Which college in Northampton, Massachusetts did Barbara Pierce (Bush) drop out of just before she married George H. W. Bush in 1945?

(490) While living in New York City, former first lady Julie Grant formed a close friendship with a one-time political adversary. Name this friend.

(491) This Republican first lady, an avid fan of the old Washington Senators, was known as the "First Lady of Baseball." Name her.

12/5/1899 ► President McKinley calls for expanding the U.S. Navy in his annual address to Congress.

(492) As televangelist and host of *The 700 Club*, this Republican established the Christian Coalition and founded the Christian Broadcast Network. Name this person who also pursued the Republican presidential nomination in 1988.

(493) Queen Victoria sent a condolence letter to which first lady after the assassination of her husband?

(494) This Republican, the son of a three-term governor of Michigan and former chairman of the Republican Governors Association, was instrumental in saving the 2002 Salt Lake City Winter Olympics by eliminating its $379 million operating budget deficit. Name him.

(495) This co-founder and executive editor of *The Weekly Standard* and co-host of *The Beltway Boys* made appearances in the films *Dave* and *Independence Day*. Name this former panelist on *The McLaughlin Group*.

(496) This Republican, born in 1957 in Key West, Florida, is a former Florida Secretary of State and a former member of the U.S. House of Representatives. However, she is most remembered for her role in the Bush-Gore vote count challenge during the 2000 presidential election. Name her.

(497) This former governor of Texas and Nixon cabinet member was wounded while riding in the motorcade when John F. Kennedy was assassinated. Name this man who changed parties and became a Republican in May 1973.

(498) This Republican is the past chairman of the National Italian American Foundation and was decorated by the government of Italy three times, including its highest decoration, "Grande Ufficiale". Name this appointee of presidents Nixon, Ford, Reagan, Bush, Sr. and Bush, Jr.

(499) Which popular and former Republican governor converted to Catholicism, the religion of his wife Columbia?

Ultimate Republican Trivia

3/7/1900 ▶ President McKinley signs the Gold Standard Act, making the value of gold the standard of value for all American currency.

(500) Which future first lady served as the first president-general of the Daughters of the American Revolution?

(501) This future first lady spent four years at an exclusive all-girl's school in Lexington, Kentucky where she and her classmates were only allowed to speak French in conversation. Name her.

(502) Born in 1958, this Roman Catholic Republican was the recipient of the John Paul II award for championing the rights of the unborn. Name this former senator from Pennsylvania, elected at age 32, many considered the most conservative member of congress.

(503) This former governor of Florida and son of a Republican president can often be heard speaking both English and Spanish. Name this convert to Roman Catholicism.

(504) This former vice presidential Chief of Staff is the co-founder and editor of *The Weekly Standard* and co-founder of the Project for the Republican Future, which is credited with helping the Republican takeover of Congress in 1994. Name him.

(505) What is the name of Republican William James "Bill" O'Reilly's evening television talk show, a program televised since 1996 that garners over an impressive 2.5 million viewers each evening?

(506) This former Secretary of State and two-term congresswoman from the state of Florida served as co-chair of George W. Bush's 2000 election campaign. Name her.

(507) Which future first lady was held up at gunpoint when she was a bank teller at age 18?

(508) This evangelical Christian leader, "born again" at age 3, is the founder of Focus on the Family (FOTF) organization and host of *Focus on the Family*, a radio show which is broadcast in more than a dozen languages and on over 7,000 stations worldwide. Name him.

(509) What is Mitt Romney's first name?

4/30/1900 ▶ **The Republican Congress passes the Organic Act, making Hawaii a U.S. territory.**

(510) Republican Mitt Romney is a former governor of which state?

(511) This Republican served on George H. W. Bush's Council on Physical Fitness and Sports. Name this two-term governor of California.

(512) Born in 1947 in Indianapolis, this Republican and former Indiana senator was the forty-fourth vice president of the United States. Name him.

(513) This former Republican mayor had his marriage to Regina Peruggi annulled claiming they were second cousins. Name this person.

(514) Born Laura Lane Welch in Midland, Texas, this only child obtained degrees from Southern Methodist University and University of Texas. Her professional career includes both teaching and librarian positions. Name her.

(515) This first lady, a librarian by profession, not only made literacy her top priority, but also helped organize the Texas Book Festival. Name her.

(516) In 1980, this Republican published a memoir in which he implied that, in 1973, Richard Nixon and Alexander Haig had planned to assassinate him if he did not resign his post as vice president. Name him.

> **IT HAPPENED ON MARCH 4, 1861**
>
> ▶ Abraham Lincoln is inaugurated as the 16th president of the United States and the first Republican president. In his address, Lincoln says that he has no intention of interfering in slavery where it exists, but that secession from the Union is illegal and will be countered with force, if necessary.

(517) Who wrote a defamating and unauthorized biography titled *Nancy Reagan: The Unauthorized Biography*?

(518) This person was present at three assassinations of Republican presidents—Abraham Lincoln in 1865, James Garfield in 1881, and William McKinley in 1901. Name him.

9/6/1901 ▶   **President McKinley is shot by anarchist Leon Czolgosz and dies one week later.**

(519) This former congressman, Pennsylvania governor, and first-ever head of Homeland Security, was the first enlisted Vietnam War combat veteran elected to the U.S. House of Representatives. Name this Bronze Star award winner.

(520) This Republican became the first woman chairman of the Republican National Committee in 1974. Name this woman from Iowa.

(521) This first lady suffered from frequent dizzy spells caused by Meniere's disease. Name her.

(522) In 1983, President Ronald Reagan appointed the first woman Secretary of Transportation. Which Republican did he appoint?

(523) In 1940, President Franklin D. Roosevelt surprised the nation when he named two prominent Republicans to his cabinet as Secretary of War and Secretary of the Navy. Name these two men.

(524) To help keep First Lady Mamie Eisenhower's mind off of flying, President Dwight D. Eisenhower had what item installed in the presidential aircraft?

(525) Which future first lady served as president of the Girl Scouts of America?

(526) What nickname did Barbara Bush's children give her to reflect her graying hair?

(527) This Republican and son of a president served as governor of Puerto Rico from 1929 to 1932 and governor general of the Philippines from 1932 to 1933. Name him.

CHAPTER 5

9/14/1901 ► **Vice President Theodore Roosevelt is sworn in as the 26th and youngest President of the United States.**

---

(528) This former Republican senator and governor of Virginia won every election he ran in from 1982 until he lost his Senate seat in November 2006. Name this person whose father was a famous NFL coach.

(529) This former speechwriter for Ronald Reagan and George H. W. Bush worked as a consultant on the TV show *The West Wing*. Name this author who is credited with penning George H. W. Bush's "a kinder, gentler nation" slogan.

(530) Which future first lady, in her youth, dated a man who later ran against her Republican husband for the presidency?

(531) Which Republican president's father was a senator from Connecticut and Wall Street financier?

(532) Therese A. Jenkins and Cora Carleton, both of Wyoming, achieved what status in the election campaign of 1892?

(533) Soon after serving as chairman of the National Republican Committee, George H. W. Bush served as chief liaison to what nation from 1974 to 1975?

(534) Mary Todd Lincoln, wife of President Abraham Lincoln, was accused by some of being a Confederate spy. For what reason was she presumed to be a Southern sympathizer?

(535) *I love You Ronnie*, a book published in 2000, contains the love letters of which presidential couple?

(536) This Republican is a highly successful American businessman, philanthropist, and mayor of New York City. In 2001, he was elected mayor on the Republican ticket after switching political parties and in 2005 he was reelected to a second term. Name him.

(537) Born in Perry, Georgia in 1947, this person became the first Republican governor of Georgia since Benjamin Conley at the end of Civil War Reconstruction in the 1870s. Name him.

---

(538) Name the title of Nancy Reagan's autobiography published in 1989.

(539) This Republican was an All-American football player at the University of Southern California and spent his entire NFL career with the Pittsburg Steelers. He is a former football and sports broadcaster for ABC Sports (1976-2005) and ran unsuccessfully for governor of Pennsylvania in 2006. Name him.

(540) This Republican served as Secretary of Education from 2001-2005. In 2000, he was named the National Alliance of Black School Educators' Superintendent of the Year and, in 2001, named the National Superintendent of the Year by the American Association of School Administrators. He was sitting with George W. Bush at the Emma E. Booker Elementary School in Florida when Bush received news of the World Trade Center terrorist attacks. Name him.

(541) Which Republican president concealed his wife's epileptic seizures?

(542) Which first lady started the "Just Say No" drug awareness campaign targeting teenagers and even appeared on the television show *Different Strokes* to advance her campaign. Name her.

(543) This first lady revealed that her husband was "the first man I ever kissed." Name her.

(544) This Republican presidential couple translated a centuries-old Latin book dating to the 16th century on mining and metals titled *De Re Metallica*. Name this couple.

(545) This woman, an assistant attorney general in the Department of Justice, became the first female to chair a Republican National Convention committee in 1928. Name her.

(546) This woman, born in New York in 1921, grew up in Maryland with an aunt and uncle while her mother pursued acting jobs. As an actress in the 1940s and 1950s, she starred in films *Donovan's Brain*, *Night into Morning*, and *Hellcats of the Navy*. Name her.

3/14/1903 ▶ **Pelican Island, Florida is declared the first federal bird reservation by President Roosevelt.**

(547) This Republican governor of Mississippi and former chairman of the Republican National Committee gained national spotlight in August 2005 after Mississippi was ravished by Hurricane Katrina. Name him.

(548) Which former governor of Florida and son of a former president completed his bachelor's degree in two and a half years?

(549) Which first lady was born Anne Francis Robbins?

(550) This superstar Boston Red Sox baseball pitcher, a devout born-again Christian and avid World War II history buff, is very vocal in his support of Republican values. Name him.

(551) Elected for the first time at age 36, this former Senate majority leader and one-time presidential candidate was the Bush-Quayle campaign director for the state of Tennessee in 1992. In addition, his great-great grandfather was one of the founders of Chattanooga, Tennessee. Name this Republican.

(552) Which first lady may have received advice by telephone from astrologer Joan Quigley concerning matters of timing for travel and special events?

(553) This former senator from Montana boasts 100% approval ratings from the National Right to Life Committee, Christian Coalition, and American Land Rights Association. Name this Republican who also boasts an outstanding 0% approval rating from the ACLU.

(554) In 1981, Sandra Day O'Connor, a former Republican state legislator and state appeals court jurist, was appointed by President Ronald Reagan to serve on the U.S. Supreme Court. Which state did she serve as a legislator and jurist?

(555) This Republican, born in 1925 in Queens, New York, was not only the first lady of the United States, but also the second lady of the United States. Her father was the president of McCall Corporation, the publisher of the popular women's magazines *Redbook* and *McCall's*. Name her.

(556) Which first lady, who had once lived in Japan, is responsible for the famous sakura (Japanese cherry trees donated by the mayor of Tokyo) found in the Washington, D.C. Tidal Basin?

(557) The wife of this Republican president held séances in the White House in an attempt to contact her dead son. Name this first lady.

(558) What cabinet post did Elizabeth Dole hold under President George H. W. Bush?

(559) This Secretary of State for Abraham Lincoln is credited with arranging the purchase of Alaska from Russia in 1867. Name this Republican.

(560) This *Wall Street Journal* editorial-page editor and 2000 Pulitzer Prize winner is a moderator of *Fox News' Journal Editorial Report*. Name this former White House fellow.

(561) Born in 1955, this former United States attorney general and chief justice of Texas was a longtime counsel to President George W. Bush until his resignation in 2007. Name this Republican.

(562) What political post did Prescott Bush, father to George H. W. Bush and grandfather of George W. Bush, hold?

(563) This five-time *New York Times* bestselling author and syndicated columnist established the *Cornell Review* and is known for her reporting of the Bill Clinton and Paula Jones scandal. Name her.

(564) This radio talk show host is known for his self-described "Excellence in Broadcasting Network" and "Advanced Conservative Studies" with "talent on loan from God." Name him.

MOVERS, SHAKERS, & FIRST LADIES

3/4/1905 ▶ Theodore Roosevelt is inaugurated for his first full-term as president.

(565) This former governor of New York privatized the World Trade Center and was instrumental in bringing the 2004 Republican National Convention to New York City. Name this Republican known for his pro-environmental policies.

(566) Which well-known and highly popular Republican governor has the middle name of Alois?

(567) This man, described by Ronald Reagan as "the number one voice for conservatism in our country," was a key force behind the Republican takeover of Congress in 1994 and was made an "honorary congressman" by a group of freshman Republicans in Congress. Name him.

(568) This Republican, born in 1950, was assistant to the president, senior advisor, and White House Deputy Chief of Staff until April 2006. Name this current Republican election strategist.

(569) What is Rudolph Giuliani's middle name?

(570) Born in Altoona, Pennsylvania to Greek Cypriot and Scots-Irish parents, this Florida governor served as state attorney general from 2003 to 2007. Name him.

(571) This person, the son of a president, joined the Union Army near the end of the Civil War and was present at Robert E. Lee's surrender at Appomattox Courthouse. Name him.

(572) Which Christian Republican is the author of novels on the coming of the *Rapture*, selling more than 60 million copies?

(573) Name the book title in which Betty Ford wrote about her personal drug and alcohol abuse.

(574) This first lady learned that her husband was not running for re-election from reading the morning newspaper. Name her.

(575) Name the motion picture film in which Nancy Reagan last appeared. (Hint: 1958)

9/2/1905 ▶ **President Roosevelt orchestrates the Portsmouth Treaty and an end to the Russo-Japanese War.**

(576) Having overcome her own challenges with pain-killers and alcohol abuse, this former first lady established a center to fight and recover from chemical dependency. Name her.

(577) This host of a nationally syndicated radio program and executive producer of a *Fox News* program helped start the African American Republican Leadership Council. Name this frequent guest host of *The Rush Limbaugh Show* and author of multiple books.

(578) Born to American parents in a Mormon colony in Mexico, this Republican and 43rd governor of Michigan ran for president in 1968, ultimately losing the Republican nomination to Richard Nixon. Name this Republican whose son became governor of Massachusetts.

(579) This Republican and former CEO of Halliburton has a federal building named for him in Casper, Wyoming. Name this one-time White House Chief of Staff under President Ford and six-term Wyoming congressman.

> **IT HAPPENED ON OCTOBER 31, 1873**
>
> ▶ The Spanish cruiser Tornado captures the American steamship Virginius which is found to be carrying arms to Cuban revolutionaries. Eight Americans and forty-five other prisoners are executed by Spanish colonial authorities as a result. The remaining American prisoners are returned and Spain pays damages in a conciliatory move to the United States.

(580) Which first lady designed her own china for the White House?

(581) What type of special needs children did Grace Coolidge, wife of Republican President Calvin Coolidge, teach and work on behalf of?

(582) This Republican, the billionaire co-founder of Amway, was ranked as the 249th richest person in the world by *Forbes* in 2007. Name this person who is a heart transplant recipient and owner of the Orlando Magic.

(583) Which first lady was nicknamed "Pat" by her father because of her Irish ancestry and for her being born on the eve of St. Patrick's Day?

(584) Previous to this first lady, pregnant women were not allowed at White House receptions. Name the Republican first lady who changed the status quo.

(585) Born in New York City in 1946, this Republican politician and author was New Jersey's first female governor (1994-2001) and was the administrator (2001-2003) of the Environmental Protection Agency under President George W. Bush. Name her.

(586) What former businessman and congressman, now governor of South Carolina, was inducted into the Taxpayers for Common Sense Hall of Fame for his stellar tax-cutting actions, particularly his 106 budget vetoes?

(587) Born in 1970, this conservative columnist, commentator, author, and host of an Internet broadcast program is a frequent guest on *Fox News* and *The O'Reilly Factor*. Name this woman whose newspaper column appears in over 200 newspapers across the country.

(588) This first lady's pastime was crocheting thousands of slippers for less fortunate people. Name her.

(589) Which first lady sometimes left a $1,000 bill, discontinued in 1969, in open view in her bedroom apparently to test the integrity of the White House staff?

(590) First Lady Barbara Bush suffered an injury while sledding at Camp David in 1991. What was her injury?

(591) Which first lady was code named "Rainbow" by the Secret Service?

(592) Who was the first Republican to win the governorship, having served two nonconsecutive terms from 1979 to 1983 and 1987 to 1991, of Texas since Reconstruction?

(593) This Republican's 1961 ghostwritten book, *The Conscience of a Conservative*, not only embodied conservative Republicanism in the early 1960s but also motivated a generation of young people to rally around conservative values. Name this Republican.

6/8/1906 ▶ President Roosevelt signs the National Monuments Act and establishes the first eighteen national monuments.

___

(594) This future first lady was a model for Powers Modeling Agency of New York. Name her.

(595) Who wrote *Millie's Book* and *C. Fred's Story*, books written from the vantage point of the family's pets?

(596) This actor and future first lady was an extra in the motion picture films *Ben Hur* and *The Great Ziegfeld*. Name her.

(597) Which non-drinking first lady was nicknamed "Lemonade Lucy" for her ban on alcohol—as well as smoking, dancing, and card playing—at all official White House functions?

(598) Born in a naval hospital in New York in 1950, this African-American political activist, author, and former diplomat ran for president in 1996, 2000, and 2008 on the Republican ticket. Name this Ambassador to the Economic and Social Council of the United Nations under President Ronald Reagan.

(599) Which Pittsburg steel tycoon of the late 1800s was a notable Republican business leader?

TOP 10
Most Populated State Capitals

	CAPITAL	STATE	POPULATION
1	Phoenix	Arizona	1,418,041
2	Indianapolis	Indiana	784,242
3	Columbus	Ohio	730,008
4	Austin	Texas	681,804
5	Boston	Massachusetts	569,165
6	Denver	Colorado	556,835
7	Nashville	Tennessee	546,719
8	Oklahoma City	Oklahoma	528,042
9	Sacramento	California	454,330
10	Atlanta	Georgia	419,122

Population does not include metropolitan area

CHAPTER

S·I·X

EVENTS & ELECTIONS

Pivotal Times in Republican History

"*I am acutely aware that you have not elected me as your president by your ballots, so I ask you to confirm me with your prayers.***"**

- GERALD FORD

"*When you are in any contest you should work as if there were - to the very last minute - a chance to lose it.***"**

- DWIGHT D. EISENHOWER

6/30/1906 ► Meat Inspection Act and Pure Food and Drug Act are signed by President Roosevelt.

(600) How many electoral votes separated George Bush and Al Gore in the 2000 presidential election? (a) 1, (b) 5, (c) 25, (d) 51, (e) 103

(601) Approximately what percentage of African-American voters did Republicans win in the 2006 elections? (a) 10%, (b) 16%, (c) 22%, (d) 31%

(602) Which former Republican president hit a hole-in-one at Seven Lakes Country Club in Palm Springs, California?

(603) This president gave artificial respiration to his Secretary of the Navy, Benjamin Tracy, after he nearly suffocated in a house fire. Name this Republican.

(604) By how many electoral votes did Rutherford B. Hayes defeat Samuel J. Tilden in the 1876 presidential election?

(605) Approximately what percentage of Catholics did George W. Bush win in the 2004 presidential election? (a) 19%, (b) 29%, (c) 40%, (d) 52%

(606) Who was Bob Dole's running mate in the 1996 presidential election?

(607) While serving in the military, which Republican suffered broken bones in both arms, one broken leg, and was knocked unconscious after ejecting from his attack aircraft?

(608) To which person did Republican President Calvin Coolidge present the Distinguished Flying Cross in 1927?

(609) Which political party, nicknamed the Bull Moose Party, did Theodore Roosevelt establish and run for president with in 1912?

(610) How many votes did James Garfield receive on the first ballot to select a presidential nominee at the Republican National Convention in 1880?

(611) What do Hubert Humphrey, George Wallace, and George McGovern have in common?

CHAPTER 6

11/9/1906 ▶ **President Roosevelt makes the first overseas trip by an American president.**

(612) Which production at Ford's Theater did Abraham Lincoln attend on the night he was shot?

(613) The Bible that both George Bush senior and junior used in their first inaugurations was used by which president in his first inauguration?

(614) Which Republican president was born in a rented apartment above a bakery in Tampico, Illinois?

(615) Approximately what percentage of active United States military personnel identify themselves as Republicans? (a) 23%, (b) 47%, (c) 57%, (d) 87%

(616) This city has a statue of William McKinley to honor the place where he was assassinated at the Pan-American Exposition. Name this city.

(617) Approximately what percentage of Hispanic-American voters did George W. Bush win in the 2004 presidential election? (a) 14%, (b) 24%, (c) 33%, (d) 44%

(618) "Experience Counts" was the slogan used by this Republican during his unsuccessful run for president. Name this man who returned and won the election eight years later.

(619) Which Republican president defeated William Jennings Bryan twice for president?

(620) Which vice president became the first "Acting President" for eight hours when the president underwent cancer surgery?

(621) In the 1984 presidential election, Ronald Reagan did not win the District of Columbia. Name the only state he did not win in the same election.

(622) On November 11, 1921, President Warren G. Harding dedicated a memorial at Arlington National Cemetery. What did he dedicate?

(623) In 1960, two prominent Republican politicians met in New York and established a joint declaration known as the "Compact of Fifth Avenue" calling for support of civil rights and increased defense spending to meet the Soviet challenge. Name these two men.

(624) This man, the first Republican presidential nominee with Jewish heritage, was a five-term United States senator from Arizona and the GOP's nominee for president in 1964. Name him.

(625) During his first campaign for president, this Republican was caught on tape calling a specific reporter a "major-league asshole." Name this president.

(626) What ailment was Abraham Lincoln suffering from when he gave his famous Gettysburg Address?

(627) In 1944, this naval officer and future Republican president was nearly thrown overboard from the U.S.S. *Monterey*, a light aircraft carrier, by a typhoon during World War II. Name him.

IT HAPPENED ON JULY 20, 1969

▶ At 4:17 P.M. the Lunar module Eagle lands on the moon. President Richard Nixon speaks to astronauts Neil Armstrong and Edwin Aldrin via radio-telephone from their location in the Sea of Tranquility.

(628) In 1983, Ronald Reagan sent U.S. troops to invade which Caribbean island nation to free American hostages and put down a Cuban-led Leftist military coup?

(629) This former Republican from Illinois ran for president as an Independent in 1980 and lost to Ronald Reagan. Name him.

(630) During Prohibition, which Republican was often seen drinking at the Belgian embassy since embassies are considered foreign soil and therefore outside of American laws?

11/16/1907 ▶ Oklahoma is admitted to the Union as the 46th state during the
Roosevelt administration.

(631) Who did Republican Bill Brock defeat in the 1970 Tennessee senatorial race?

(632) Charles Guiteau, a Washington lawyer, was hanged on June 30, 1882 at the "Washington Bastille," part of the Washington Jail. What was his crime that resulted in a death sentence?

(633) Which Republican candidate for president in 1936 lost to Franklin D. Roosevelt 523 to 8 in electoral votes, marking the largest victory margin in the Electoral College since James Monroe in 1820?

(634) In the 2004 presidential election, George W. Bush gained two states and lost one state as compared to the 2000 presidential election. Which two states did he gain and which one state did he lose?

(635) Which president dispatched American armed forces to the Middle East within days of the invasion of Kuwait and subsequently drove Saddam Hussein out of Kuwait in the first Gulf War?

(636) On April 5, 2006, this university renamed its law school the Sandra Day O'Connor College of Law. Name this university.

(637) Which newspaper printed the famous, but inaccurate, banner headline "Dewey Defeats Truman" the morning after the 1948 presidential election?

(638) In 1975, President Gerald Ford dispatched U.S. Marines to rescue captured Americans after their ship was seized by the Khmer Rouge. Name the ship for which this international crisis is named.

(639) Which conviction against George W. Bush was revealed only days before the 2000 presidential election?

(640) Robert Dole defeated which millionaire publisher for the Republican nomination in the 1996 presidential election campaign?

(641) What was the famous slogan used by Dwight D. Eisenhower during his 1952 presidential campaign?

(642) After his defeat to John F. Kennedy in the 1960 presidential election, Richard Nixon ran unsuccessfully for which state office in 1962?

(643) Which tiny Pacific island, now a United States territory, was acquired during the presidency of Republican William McKinley following the Spanish-American War?

(644) In 1957, the Republican National Committee created a southern arm of its organization and launched an "operation" to expand the GOP base south of the Mason-Dixie line. What was the name for this operation?

(645) Which former governor of New York is the only Republican nominee to lose two successive presidential elections?

(646) Approximately what percentage of gay and lesbian Americans identify themselves as Republicans? (a) 3%, (b) 9%, (c) 13%, (d) 23%

(647) In 1984, Ronald Reagan easily defeated presidential candidate Walter Mondale. Who was Mondale's vice presidential running mate?

(648) During the 1988 presidential election, the major opponent of Republican George H. W. Bush was often times referred to as the governor of "Taxachusetts." Name this opponent.

(649) Which hip-hop Latino entertainer and singer performed at the inaugural party for George W. Bush in 2001?

(650) In 1992, this man announced his candidacy for president on Larry King's call-in show. Soon thereafter his popularity surged and he jumped ahead of both George H. W. Bush and Bill Clinton in the polls. Name him.

(651) In which presidential election was the first-ever Republican National Convention held in New York City?

(652) Which opponent from Massachusetts did George H. W. Bush defeat in the 1988 presidential election?

5/30/1908 ▶ The Republican Congress permits banks to issue money based on commercial paper and government bonds.

---

(653) This future Republican president, while serving in the Third Fleet in the South Pacific during World War II, nearly died in December 1944 when a typhoon struck killing 800 sailors. Name him.

(654) Using a crude metal detector called an "induction balance," this famous inventor attempted to find the bullet lodged in President James Garfield after he was shot. He was unsuccessful because the president was placed on a bed with metal springs that disrupted the metal detector. Name this inventor.

(655) Which major party candidate did Dwight D. Eisenhower defeat twice for president in 1952 and 1956?

(656) Upon which hill in Cuba did Theodore Roosevelt lead his Rough Riders on a charge?

(657) In addition to Abraham Lincoln, who did John Wilkes Booth plan to assassinate that night at Ford's Theater?

(658) This Republican and former Secretary of Transportation ran for president in 2000 but withdrew, largely due to inadequate fund-raising, in October 1999 before any of the primaries. Name this Republican.

(659) This New Yorker was appointed Commander of the Army of the Potomac by President Abraham Lincoln and later opposed Lincoln in the 1864 presidential election. Name him.

(660) During the presidency of William McKinley, which American admiral defeated the Spanish Navy in Manila harbor in the Spanish-American War?

---

(661) Which Republican president was the first to address a joint session of British Parliament?

(662) In 1907, President Theodore Roosevelt dedicated which Gothic cathedral?

(663) During his re-election campaign, this Republican used the slogan "Morning in America." Name this president.

(664) During the presidency of William McKinley, which U.S. Navy battleship was sunk while docked in Havana, Cuba thus triggering Congress to declare war on Spain?

(665) The body of which president was nearly stolen on the night of November 7, 1876?

(666) Who was President of the United States during the first moon landing and cease fire in Vietnam?

(667) Which niece of Theodore Roosevelt did he "give away" in marriage?

(668) Ronald Reagan kicked off the 1982 World's Fair in which American city?

(669) Who did George W. Bush defeat to win the 1994 Texas gubernatorial race?

(670) In December 1898, which Caribbean commonwealth island did the United States formally annex while William McKinley was president?

(671) "Are you better off than you were four years ago?" was asked by which highly popular Republican during his run for president?

(672) In April 1993, Kuwaiti authorities uncovered a plot to assassinate a former American leader while he visited Kuwait with his family. In response, President Bill Clinton ordered a cruise missile attack against the Iraqi Intelligence Service in Bagdad for its lead role in the plot. Which American leader was targeted by the Iraqis?

10/31/1912 ▶ **Vice President John Sherman dies and is replaced by President Taft with Nicholas Butler as his new running mate.**

(673) In 1964, this Republican made his formal declaration for president and promised "a choice, not an echo" against Lyndon Johnson. Name him.

(674) Which two Republicans were technically president on the same day since the oath of office for one of these two men was held in private before the formal inauguration and therefore the end of the term for the current president?

(675) Which presidential election was the tighter race—Bush/Gore in 2000 or Bush/Kerry in 2004?

(676) Which Republican was in the White House when the 27th Amendment and most recent amendment to the United States Constitution was ratified making all salary increases for members of Congress effective only after the next general election?

(677) Who was the first Republican to win the Catholic vote in a presidential election?

(678) Which two Republican presidents were born in log cabins?

TOP 10		
MOST TOTAL SEATS BY STATE IN THE HOUSE		
	STATE	SEATS
1	California	53
2	Texas	32
3	New York	29
4	Florida	25
5	Pennsylvania	19
6	Illinois	19
7	Ohio	18
8	Michigan	15
9	New Jersey	13
t10	North Carolina	13
t10	Georgia	13

(679) Name the two "cliffhanger" states in the 2000 presidential election and 2004 presidential election.

(680) King Tut, the pet dog of a Republican president, was featured prominently in campaign promotional materials to showcase this president's warmer side. Name this president.

(681) "Back from Elba" clubs were established to spur which former Republican to run again for president?

(682) During the presidency of Ronald Reagan, 241 American Marines lost their lives when a suicide driver exploded his truck in the compound where the Marines were sleeping. In which distant country did this tragic event occur?

(683) On which Christian holiday was Abraham Lincoln shot?

(684) This Republican shattered his thigh bone while participating in a celebrity baseball game. Name him.

(685) After Abraham Lincoln was shot at Ford's Theater he was rushed across the street to a boarding house for actors. In whose previously occupied room was Lincoln placed?

(686) Who did Lloyd M. Bentsen, Jr. defeat in the 1970 Texas senatorial race?

(687) Which two major candidates did Ronald Reagan defeat in the 1980 and 1984 presidential elections?

(688) Which Republican referred to Ronald Reagan's initiative to cut taxes as part of supply-side economics as "voodoo economics"?

(689) What is the name of the theater in Washington, D.C. where President Abraham Lincoln was shot?

(690) During his election campaign, which Republican president used "Born in the U.S.A." by Bruce Springsteen as his theme song until Springsteen made a fuss?

(691) On January 20, 1981, Ronald Reagan was inaugurated as the 40th President of the United States. On that same day, which country freed 52 Americans held hostage?

(692) "Let us have peace" was the campaign slogan of which Republican president?

(693) What was the name of the airplane used by Ronald Reagan during his 1980 presidential campaign?

(694) This Republican vice president lost his bid for president but won the White House eight years later. Name him.

(695) In what year was the Republican National Convention held at Joe Louis Arena in Detroit?

(696) Which Republican president referred to America as "a thousand points of light in a broad and peaceful sky"?

(697) While playing with his "poker cabinet," which president gambled away an entire set of White House china dating back to President Benjamin Harrison?

(698) On May 7, 1960, the United States admitted that one of its aircraft was shot down over the U.S.S.R. while on a spying mission. Four days later President Eisenhower, while defending such flights as "distasteful but vital," canceled all future missions. What type of aircraft was shot down?

(699) Name the bride and groom, both children of Republican presidents, married in 1968 by Norman Vincent Peale, preacher and author of the book *The Power of Positive Thinking.*

(700) This man was permanently disabled when a bullet passed through his brain during the assassination attempt of President Ronald Reagan in 1981. Name him.

(701) Who are the three major candidates George W. Bush defeated in the 2000 presidential election?

(702) Which vice president became president upon the assassination of Abraham Lincoln? (Hint: Not a Republican)

(703) In 1892, the birthday of this president became an official national holiday. Name this president.

(704) Approximately what percentage of full-time college faculty identify themselves as Republicans? (a) 15%, (b) 25%, (c) 50%, (d) 65%

4/20/1921 ► **The Republican Congress authorizes payment of $25 million to Colombia for the loss of Panama.**

(705) Strom Thurmond of South Carolina was a presidential nominee of which political party, nicknamed the "Dixiecats," in the 1948 election?

(706) Which president was known for the expression, "To replace a national frown with a national smile"?

(707) The record for the most ballots needed to select a presidential nominee at a Republican National Convention is 36. Name the Republican nominated.

(708) Which person was stalked, but escaped unharmed, by John Wilkes Booth on the very day Booth shot President Abraham Lincoln?

(709) In 1901, the Secret Service became the official presidential body guard in response to what event?

(710) Which city has hosted the most Republican National Conventions?

(711) Name the man who shot Ronald Reagan on March 30, 1981.

Theodore Roosevelt and family

CHAPTER
VII
S·E·V·E·N

JOHN S. McCAIN III

2008 Republican Presidential Nominee

"*I believe we have the votes and we believe we have the momentum.***"**

- JOHN McCAIN

"*I am fully prepared to be commander in chief... I don't need on-the-job training.***"**

- JOHN McCAIN

6/10/1921 ► **Bureau of the Budget and General Accounting Office established by Budget and Accounting Act signed by President Harding.**

(712) In April 2008, John McCain called for a summer tax holiday amendment between Memorial Day and Labor Day 2008. What specific tax holiday did he propose?

(713) In which two areas of the United States does John McCain support an appeal of the ban on oil exploration and production?

(714) In 2002, John McCain voted in favor of a bill allowing re-importation of what product from Canada?

(715) According to John McCain, which two Supreme Court justices will he use as models if he should need to nominate a justice to the high court?

(716) John McCain was shot down on October 26, 1967 over which of the following countries? (a) North Vietnam, (b) South Vietnam, (c) Cambodia, (d) Laos

(717) What is John McCain's ethnic ancestry?

(718) In 2007, John McCain was the lead Republican on which tax freedom act involving commerce?

(719) On which television show in February 2007 did John McCain announce he would indeed seek the presidency in 2008?

(720) In September 2006, did John McCain vote "yes" or "no" on a bill to build a fence along the Mexican border?

(721) In February 2007, the U.S. senate approved a bill increasing the minimum wage to $7.25 an hour. Did John McCain vote in favor or against this bill?

JOHN S. MCCAIN III

(722) In 1954, John McCain graduated from Episcopal High School. Name the state where this school is located.

(723) What theory explaining the beginning of human civilization does John McCain support the teaching of in schools to provide students with "all points of view"?

(724) John S. McCain was born on August 29, 1936 at the Coco Solo air base hospital. Where specifically was he born?

IT HAPPENED ON DECEMBER 29, 1900

▶ Denmark agrees in principle to sell the Dutch West Indies, later renamed the U.S. Virgin Islands, to the United States during the presidency of William McKinley. The transfer of ownership does not occur until 1917 when additional negotiations are held and Congress authorizes the $25 million payment.

(725) Does John McCain, an evidenced by his April 1998 vote, support or oppose allowing personal retirement accounts?

(726) In 2006, John McCain introduced the Federal Funding Accountability and Transparency Act bill with three other senators, including Tom Coburn (R-Oklahoma) and Tom Carper (D-Delaware). Name the fourth senator.

(727) Did John McCain vote in support or opposition to confirm John Roberts and Samuel Alito to the United States Supreme Court?

(728) What is the name of John McCain's wife?

(729) John McCain was named one of "America's 10 Best Senators" in 2006. Name the magazine giving him this recognition.

(730) Which profession did John McCain's youngest son, James McCain, join in September 2006?

(731) How many years did John McCain serve as a naval aviator?

(732) Given his votes in 2004 and 2005, does John McCain support or oppose banning lawsuits against gun manufacturers for gun violence?

8/3/1923 ▶ **Calvin C. Coolidge is sworn in as the 30th President of the United States.**

(733) While in captivity John McCain's captors gave him what nickname after they learned his father was an admiral in the United States Navy?

(734) John McCain received a sizable advance from Random House for his book, *Faith of My Fathers* (2000). McCain gave half the money to his staff and the other half to whom?

(735) True or False. While in captivity in North Vietnam, John McCain was offered an early release when his captors learned that his father was an admiral but John McCain declined the offer citing military policy of releasing prisoners in the order in which they were captured.

(736) What was the name for John McCain's 2000 presidential campaign bus tour?

(737) Which aliment does John McCain suffer from that has motivated him to be active in promoting awareness of skin cancer?

(738) What experience was chronicled in *The Nightingale's Song*, a book by Robert Timberg?

Capture of John McCain

(739) In May 1999, did John McCain vote "yes" or "no" on a bill declaring memorial prayers and religious symbols are OK in schools?

(740) What assignment, starting in 1968, did John McCain's father, John S. McCain, Jr., hold during the Vietnam War?

(741) Why was John McCain nicknamed John Wayne McCain by his Naval Academy classmates?

CHAPTER 7

(742) In what year did Senator John McCain introduce an amendment to the Defense Appropriations bill that prohibits cruel, inhumane, and degrading treatment of all detainees held in Department of Defense custody, including those of the CIA? (a) 2000, (b) 2002, (c) 2005, (d) 2008

(743) In March 2007, did John McCain vote "yes" or "no" on a bill to repeal the Alternative Minimum Tax?

(744) During naval flight training school, John McCain survived a close call crash. Where did this crash occur?

(745) Which nickname did John McCain receive in response to working a relentless schedule as a senator?

(746) Which attack aircraft was John McCain piloting when he was shot down?

(747) Which instrument did John McCain once play during a campaign stop in June 1999 in rural New Hampshire for more than 2,000 supporters?

(748) What is John McCain's position on the sovereignty of Israel?

(749) In June 2007, did John McCain vote "yes" or "no" on a bill declaring English as the official language of the U.S. government?

(750) Aboard which ship did John McCain survive a terrible explosion when his aircraft was hit by a missile accidentally fired from another aircraft?

(751) John McCain's great-aunt is said to be a descendent of which legendary Scottish king?

(752) Who described John McCain as a "wise ass" and "older than dirt" and even likened him to Luke Skywalker during his bid for the 2000 presidential nomination?

(753) In February 2008, John McCain supported which stimulus package?

(754) What percentage of the time has John McCain voted with Republicans? (a) 43, (b) 59, (c) 87%, (d) 100

(755) What moral position did John McCain support with his votes in 1999, 2000, 2003, 2006, and 2007?

(756) In addition to the Senate Committee on Commerce, Science, and Transportation, of which two other Senate Committees is John McCain the Ranking Member?

(757) Which of the following military awards did John McCain receive? (a) Bronze Star, (b) Distinguished Flying Cross, (c) Legion of Merit, (d) Purple Heart, (e) Silver Star

(758) In which year did John S. McCain graduate from the U.S. Naval Academy? (a) 1949, (b) 1958, (c) 1964, (d) 1970

IT HAPPENED ON OCTOBER 22, 1986

▶ President Ronald Reagan ushers in the most comprehensive revision to the tax code in more than forty years when he signs the Tax Reform Act. Tax rates are lowered for most taxpayers.

(759) In what year was John McCain first elected to the United States House of Representatives to serve Arizona's then-first district?

(760) What does the McCain-Feingold legislation (passed on May 20, 2002) attempt to reform?

(761) Which state does John McCain represent in the United States Senate?

(762) What nickname did the media bestow on John McCain in response to his reputation for sometimes crossing party lines and instead taking independent positions?

(763) John McCain's family lineage can be traced back to the American Revolution. What assignment did John Young, an early John McCain ancestor, hold during that war?

(764) In *Faith of My Fathers*, a book by John McCain, what did John McCain do when angered as a child?

(765) In June 2006, John McCain voted yes on recommending a Constitutional ban on what type of desecration?

(766) After being shot down by a surface-to-air missile on his 23rd bombing mission on October 26, 1967, John McCain was held captive nearly six years at the infamous Hoa Lo prison, much of it in solitary confinement. By what other dubious name was this prison known as?

(767) What historic event did John McCain's grandfather, John S. McCain Sr., witness while serving aboard the U.S.S. *Missouri* on September 2, 1945?

(768) On which side did most of John McCain's ancestors fight during the American Civil War?

(769) John McCain is a member of an exclusive club in Washington, D.C. that honors the birthday of Confederate General Robert E. Lee with an annual banquet each January. Name the club.

(770) John McCain and his wife Cindy adopted their youngest daughter, Bridget, after discovering her in an orphanage in Bangladesh. Which famous Christian woman ran this orphanage?

(771) John McCain is one of two Republican Vietnam War veterans currently serving in the United States Senate. Name the other Republican holding this distinction as of 2008?

(772) Which religion does John McCain practice?

CHAPTER E·I·G·H·T

MISCELLANEA & ODDITIES

Little Known Facts and the Strange But True

> ❝*Four fifths of all our troubles in this life would disappear if we would only sit down and keep still.*❞
>
> - CALVIN COOLIDGE

> ❝*Terrorist attacks can shake the foundations of our biggest buildings, but they cannot touch the foundation of America. These acts shatter steel, but they cannot dent the steel of American resolve.*❞
>
> - GEORGE W. BUSH

(773) Before he became a hero of the Civil War, this future Republican sold firewood in St. Louis to make ends meet. Name him.

(774) While attending Yale Law School, which two sports programs did Gerald Ford coach?

(775) How many combat missions did George H. W. Bush fly in as a naval aviator during World War II? (a) 19, (b) 29, (c) 46, (d) 58

(776) The first wife of this future president died of Bright's disease, a kidney ailment, only two days after giving birth to their first child. This disease had not been diagnosed as it was masked by the pregnancy. Name this Republican president.

(777) Which Republican president nicknamed his son "Tad" because he thought his son looked like a tadpole as he was born with a cleft palate?

(778) Ronald Reagan served three years in the U.S. Army during World War II. For what reason was he not authorized for combat duty?

(779) The mother of which president lived with him at the White House?

(780) At age seven, this future Republican president spent several months living with his uncle on the Osage Reservation in Oklahoma Territory. Name him.

(781) Ronald Reagan made his screen debut in what 1937 motion picture film?

(782) What did John Wilkes Booth shout out after shooting Abraham Lincoln?

(783) Which Republican president was named for a hero of Greek mythology?

(784) The paternal grandfather of which noted Republican president was killed by Native American Indians?

7/9/1970 ▶ President Nixon proposes the creation of the U.S. Environmental Protection Agency.

---

(785) Which Republican president had a horseshoe pit installed on the White House lawn?

(786) What name did George H. W. Bush give to each of the fighter aircraft he flew during World War II as a naval aviator?

> ### IT HAPPENED ON AUGUST 2, 1923
>
> ▶ President Warren G. Harding dies after contracting ptomaine poisoning, which progresses into pneumonia, while on his cross-country "Voyage of Understanding" tour. The formal announcement claims Harding died of a stroke, but Naval physicians point to a heart attack. No conclusive cause has since been determined.

(787) During the Civil War, which major city on the Mississippi River did Union General Ulysses Grant be-siege and capture, leading to his significant fame?

(788) Which Republican president had his home street address number changed from 666 to 668 because of the satanic connotations?

(789) Theodore Roosevelt was known as an outdoorsy and rough fellow. From whom then did he buy his spurs, belt buckle, and Bowie knife?

(790) Which evangelical leader once accused Nickelodeon of creating a gay cartoon character in *SpongeBob SquarePants*?

(791) How many copies of the Gettysburg Address, written by Abraham Lincoln himself, exist today?

(792) Which Republican president was named for his great-grandfather, one of the signers of the Declaration of Independence?

(793) Born in 1931, this flamboyant and highly controversial boxing promoter, recognized for his wild hairstyle, actively promoted George W. Bush during the 2004 presidential election and even attended the Republican National Convention in New York that same year. Name him.

(794) Name the 1951 movie in which Ronald Reagan co-starred with a chimpanzee.

8/12/1972 ▶ **President Nixon authorizes the final withdrawal of U.S. troops from South Vietnam.**

(795) Arthur Eisenhower, brother of Dwight D. Eisenhower, roomed with a future American president while in a Kansas City boarding house. Who was his roommate?

(796) Which Republican senator wrote *Worth Fighting for: A Memoir, Why Courage Matters: The Way to a Braver Life,* and *Character Is Destiny?*

(797) Which Republican president was known as the "Idol of Ohio"?

(798) How many siblings did President Benjamin Harrison have?

(799) Beau Bridges and Ron Silver played Richard Nixon and Henry Kissinger, respectively, in which 1996 motion picture film?

(800) The fall of which Republican president was the underlying theme of the motion picture film *All the President's Men?*

(801) President Herbert Hoover called his death in 1931 "a national loss." Name this legendary head football coach who led the Fighting Irish to consecutive undefeated records in his final two seasons.

(802) For which Republican president are toy logs named?

(803) This president liked fishing, while wearing a tie, because "all men are created equal before the fish." Name this Republican.

(804) In 1974, Ronald Reagan purchased a 688-acre ranch in the mountains east of Santa Barbara, California. Name this ranch.

(805) This Republican and former member of the Warren Commission that investigated the assassination of John F. Kennedy wrote the book *Portrait of the Assassin.* Name him.

CHAPTER 8

(806) This future Republican president hosted the television series *General Electric Theater* (1954-1962) and *Death Valley Days* (1962-1965). Name him.

(807) The Detroit Lions and Green Bay Packers offered tryouts to this future Republican president, but he turned them down to study and coach at Yale. Name him.

(808) Which Republican president was known for his unique ability to recite long passages from William Shakespeare?

(809) What is the title of George H. W. Bush's 1988 autobiography?

(810) Born in 1956 in Bejucal, Cuba, this Academy Award-nominated American actor appeared in such films as *The Godfather: Part III*, *The Untouchables*, and *Ocean's Eleven*. Name this Cuban-American Republican.

(811) Which design motif honoring a fallen president appears on the U.S. one-cent coin and five-dollar bill?

(812) *Personal Memoirs* is a lengthy two-volume set published by Mark Twain and written by a Republican president while he was dying of throat cancer. Name this Republican whose family earned $450,000 from the royalties.

(813) Which presidential couple was known to communicate in sign language when they wanted to keep their conversation private?

(814) The father of this early Republican president arranged for his appointment to West Point without his knowledge. Name this future president who at the time had no intention of a military career.

(815) Grover G. Norquist, founder and head of Americans for Tax Reform and coauthor of the "Contract With America", unsuccessfully attempted to get the picture of which president placed on the $10 bill claiming that a president deserved the honor instead of non-president Alexander Hamilton. Name the president.

(816) Ronald Reagan and Nancy Davis (Reagan) first appeared together in which 1950s motion picture film?

(817) Just before giving a campaign speech in Milwaukee, this former president was shot in the chest in an assassination attempt. Fortunately, the bullet hit a metal spectacle case in his breast pocket and deflected away from his heart and lungs and lodged in a rib. Name this man who gave the speech even with a bullet lodged in his chest.

(818) This Harvard-educated president wrote *The Winning of the West*, *Hunting Trip of a Ranchman*, and *Rough Riders*. Name this much-published Republican.

IT HAPPENED ON JANUARY 31, 1865

▶ The Republican-controlled U.S House of Representatives approves, along with the support of President Abraham Lincoln, the 13th Amendment to the United States Constitution. This amendment ends slavery in all states and territories of the United States. The amendment is ratified on December 18, 1865 by a two-thirds majority of states and therefore becomes law.

---

(819) Which Republican president was inflicted with and later died from Bright's disease, a kidney ailment that was fatal during his lifetime?

(820) Which American president dubbed himself "the jinx of the links" in reference to his golf game?

(821) Theodore Roosevelt always carried six pairs of this item into combat during the Spanish-American War. Name the item.

(822) Which Republican president grew up in Dixon, Illinois?

(823) Which early Republican president said, "You can fool all of the people part of the time and part of the people all the time, but you cannot fool all the people all the time"?

(824) Which four Republican presidents were given their mother's maiden name as their middle name?

(825) As a lifeguard and swim coach, this future president saved a total of 77 people from drowning near his hometown in Illinois. Name him.

(826) Which actor played Richard Nixon in the 1995 motion picture film *Nixon* produced by Oliver Stone?

(827) What was Ulysses S. Grant's birth name?

(828) Which Republican president had a strong taste for pork rinds with Tabasco sauce?

(829) Which organization did Ulysses S. Grant, Theodore Roosevelt, William Howard Taft, Dwight D. Eisenhower, Richard M. Nixon, Ronald Reagan, and George H. W. Bush once belong? (Hint: Charlton Heston)

(830) In how many motion picture films did Ronald Reagan appear during his career of nearly 30 years? (a) 23, (b) 31, (c) 45, (d) 53

(831) Which former Republican president has a facial scar resulting from an accident while playing soccer in prep school?

(832) Which Republican called "Dixie", a favorite song of many Southerners, "one of the best tunes I ever heard"?

(833) Watching TV Westerns and eating TV dinners with his wife was the ideal evening event for which president?

(834) William Howard Taft was appointed governor-general of which newly acquired territory?

(835) Harry S. Truman and one other president were noted piano players. Name the second president who even gifted a Steinway piano to Truman.

(836) Name the Louisiana Republican gubernatorial candidate who was a former leader of the Ku Klux Klan.

(837) In 1982, this man received a jury verdict of "not guilty" for reason of insanity for his attempted assassination of President Ronald Reagan in 1981. Name him.

(838) Which Republican was the last American president to smoke a pipe?

(839) During the Civil War, future Republican president Benjamin Harrison was given a nickname in reference to his diminutive stature by those who served under him. What was the nickname?

(840) Which son of President Franklin D. Roosevelt became a member of the Republican Party?

(841) Although President William Howard Taft did not serve in the military, he was still buried in Arlington National Cemetery. Why was this permitted?

(842) When this future president was married, his parents did not attend because they disapproved of the bride's family for owning slaves. Name this Republican.

(843) Which Republican is the only president to be ambidextrous?

(844) What nickname did George H. W. Bush receive for his advocacy of population control while a congressman during the 1960s?

(845) Actor Brian Keith played which Republican president in the 1975 motion picture film *The Wind and the Lion*?

(846) Only two presidents (one being John F. Kennedy) are buried at Arlington National Cemetery. Name the Republican who is buried close to Abraham Lincoln's son Robert?

(847) While in college, which future Republican president made ends meet by washing dishes at his fraternity house and by working as a lifeguard?

(848) Theodore Roosevelt was nearly blind in his left eye due to trauma inflicted from playing a particular sport. Name this sport.

9/8/1974 ▶ President Ford pardons Richard Nixon of all criminal charges related to the Watergate scandal.

(849) Which Republican president had the White House swimming pool filled in (only to be dug up by Gerald Ford) to provide more room for the press to stand when covering events?

(850) Which American president was the first to wear a full beard in office?

(851) Name Richard Nixon's pet dog that was made famous by a television speech.

(852) What is the name of the exclusive club/society George H. W. Bush and George W. Bush joined while at Yale?

(853) Which vegetable did President George H. W. Bush prohibit from the menu on Air Force One given his disgust for having to eat it as a child?

(854) This Republican's mother and wife of four years both died on Valentine's Day in 1884 of unrelated causes. Name him.

(855) Which Republican president fathered a child at age 64?

(856) In 1984, Maureen Reagan, daughter of Ronald Reagan, told reporters that she and her husband saw the ghost of a past president in the White House. Which president did they claim to see?

(857) Ulysses S. Grant became stricken with throat cancer ten years after leaving the White House. What substance did he use to swab his throat, eventually becoming addicted to it?

REPUBLICAN TOP 10
Most Conservative Senator

	SENATOR	SCORE
1	DeMint, Jim, R-S.C.	93.8
2	Allard, Wayne, R-Colo.	92.5
3	Burr, Richard, R-N.C.	92.2
4	Cornyn, John, R-Texas	91.2
5	Enzi, Michael, R-Wyo.	90.8
6	Bunning, Jim, R-Ky.	89.8
7	Isakson, Johnny, R-Ga.	87.5
8	Inhofe, James, R-Okla.	86.7
9	McConnell, Mitch, R-Ky.	86.5
10	Sessions, Jeff, R-Ala.	85.8

Source: National Journal, 2007

(858) This Republican was nicknamed "Gloomy Gus" as a student at Duke University Law School. Name him.

(859) How many Republican presidents have been only children?

(860) Which president and his family had a one-legged chicken for a pet?

(861) In 1938, former president Herbert Hoover met a European leader he described as "partly insane." Which leader did he meet?

(862) For what reason did Ulysses S. Grant change his name from Hiram Ulysses Grant?

(863) This Republican president often went by "Dutch", a nickname given by his father. Name him.

(864) In which military unit did President George W. Bush serve as a pilot from 1968 to 1973?

(865) This Republican president gave his wife a ring inscribed with the expression, "Love is eternal." Name him.

(866) Which future Republican president was charged with disorderly conduct for stealing a Christmas tree while in college?

(867) Before this Republican became president, he served as "Chief U.S. Liaison to China" and American ambassador to the United Nations. Name him.

(868) Which of the Seven Wonders of the World did future Republican president Theodore Roosevelt climb?

(869) Rudolph Giuliani appeared as himself in what movie with Jack Nicholson and Adam Sandler?

(870) The son of this future Republican president died from an infection starting in his toe caused by a blister suffered while playing tennis. Name the president.

(871) Why was the Secret Service enlisted to trap squirrels for President Dwight D. Eisenhower?

(872) Five future presidents served in the military during the Civil War. Which Republican was the only future president to be wounded?

(873) Martha (Mittie) Bulloch, a Georgian plantation belle and the mother of a Republican president, openly supported the Confederacy during the Civil War. Name this president.

(874) In which state was George H. W. Bush born?

(875) In the Hall of Presidents at Walt Disney World in Florida, a robotic Republican president stands up and makes a presentation. Name the president.

(876) Which candy was the favorite of President Ronald Reagan?

(877) Which character did Ronald Reagan play in the 1940 motion picture film *Knute Rockne, All American*?

(878) In his younger years, which Republican president was nicknamed "Little Pop" or "Poppy"?

(879) Movie star Gregory Peck was used in commercials to protest the nomination by President Ronald Reagan of which justice to the Supreme Court?

(880) After completing his service in the U.S. Navy, George H. W. Bush graduated from which university in two and a half years?

(881) Referred to as the "Queen of Latin Pop," this Cuban-American singer and songwriter boasts five Grammy Awards, numerous number one hits, and over 90 million albums sold worldwide. Name this registered Republican.

(882) Which famous golf course has a cottage named for Dwight D. Eisenhower to honor the many times he played there? (Hint: Georgia)

1/20/1981 ▶ **Ronald W. Reagan is inaugurated as the 40th President of the United States.**

(883) To which wealthy American did Ulysses S. Grant sell most of his military equipment, including uniforms and medals, to help pay down his large outstanding debts?

(884) Born on August 10, 1874, this Republican was the first American president to be born west of the Mississippi River. Name him.

IT HAPPENED ON DECEMBER 10, 1898

▶ The Spanish-American War is concluded with the Treaty of Paris. The treaty requires Spain to cede Puerto Rico and Guam to the United States. Temporary control of Cuba is gained by the United States as is control of the Philippines for a $20 million payment to Spain.

(885) Ulysses S. Grant acquired a slave from his father-in-law in 1848 after his marriage to Julia Dent of St. Louis. What did Grant do with the slave?

(886) Which future president covered the Chicago Cubs and Big Ten football as a broadcast announcer for radio station WHO in Des Moines, Iowa?

(887) What section of the newspaper did Ronald Reagan typically read first?

(888) Which president used the alias "Walter Gerguson" instead of his real name to play the stock market?

(889) Which Republican president was born Leslie Lynch King but later renamed after his adoptive father, a paint salesman?

(890) President Richard Nixon enlisted the help of a legendary music performer as an honorary special agent in the administration's war on drugs. Name him.

(891) This independent senator from Connecticut received a kiss from President George W. Bush following the 2005 State of the Union Address. Name this senator and outspoken supporter of both the Iraq War and John McCain for president.

MISCELLANEA & ODDITIES

3/20/1981 ► President Reagan is shot in the chest by John Hinckley, Jr.

(892) Which president was self-described as a "Plain Hoosier Colonel" but was later promoted to general during the Civil War?

(893) Which woman became the first child of a president to appear nude in a magazine?

(894) What was the name of the golden retriever President Gerald Ford often kept in the Oval Office?

(895) Prior to entering politics, in which military campaign did Abraham Lincoln participate in a group led by Zachary Taylor?

(896) How many Republican presidents were the eldest sons in their families?

(897) Which American president needed to shave at least twice each day due to his heavy beard?

(898) The 18th, 19th, and 20th presidents of the United States were all Republicans and all born in the same state. Name this state.

(899) Which future Republican president was the supreme commander of all allied armed forces in Europe during World War II?

(900) This biweekly magazine, founded by William F. Buckley, Jr. in 1955, is considered by many to be America's most widely read and influential Republican/conservative magazine. Name this publication with over 150,000 subscribers.

(901) The son of which Republican president had two pet alligators that wandered loose in the White House?

(902) Sales of this electronic device soared 40% after Ronald Reagan got his first one. What is this device?

(903) This president enjoyed eating cottage cheese smothered in ketchup. Name him.

(904) Louis C. Tiffany was enlisted by which Republican president to redecorate and furnish the White House?

8/5/1981 ▶ **President Reagan dismisses 13,000 air traffic controllers for going on strike and violating federal law.**

(905) Which state adopted the red carnation as its state flower due in large part to President William McKinley wearing it on his lapel for good luck?

(906) In 1985, this Republican paid $300 to become a life member of the National Rifle Association only to withdraw his membership in 2005 over what he called anti-government rhetoric from the NRA. Name him.

(907) For what reason was the broadcast of the Oscars in 1981 delayed? (Hint: former movie star)

(908) This Republican president received a scar above his right eye from a fight with would-be thieves. Name him.

(909) Which European leader did President George W. Bush attempt to give a back rub to during the 2006 G-8 summit?

(910) Which Republican served as the city attorney for Indianapolis before entering politics?

(911) The Restigouche Salmon Club, the oldest and perhaps most exclusive fishing club in North America, boasted which American president and avid fisherman as a member?

(912) In 1849, Abraham Lincoln was offered the governorship of which U.S. territory that he subsequently declined?

(913) Which future Republican president played football at the United States Military Academy and suffered a knee injury that ended his football career?

(914) Who was the first American president to have his voice recorded, the first to travel in a submarine, and last to ride in a carriage to his inauguration?

(915) The five brothers of this Republican president all had the same nickname. Name this president and his nickname.

(916) Which Republican was the first president to take the oath of office in the White House?

(917) Which president smoked nearly 20 cigars each day, a habit that ultimately led to his death from throat cancer?

(918) Which American president was raised in Poland?

(919) In 1858, this future president abandoned farming and attempted, but failed, to make a career of real estate sales in St. Louis. Name him.

(920) To ensure this president could have fresh milk, a cow was kept on the White House lawn. Name this president.

(921) Which future president, along with other investors, purchased the Texas Rangers for $86 million making this Republican the first and only president to own a professional baseball team?

(922) While at West Point, which future Republican president rolled his own cigarettes and later smoked four packets per day?

(923) As a senator, this Republican from Ohio voted in favor of Prohibition. However, as president he kept liquor at the White House in violation of the law. Name him.

(924) Which American president wore a white vest and red carnation in his lapel nearly every day for good luck?

(925) This presidential canine, along with her pups, made the cover of *Life* magazine. Name this Bush family dog.

(926) The largest subspecies of American elk is named for a Republican president. Name the president.

(927) "I wish we could make him president" was said of Herbert Hoover by which future American president in 1921?

(928) Abraham Lincoln became a Republican in 1856. Which political party was he a member of until that time?

(929) To which actress was Ronald Reagan married from 1940 to 1948?

(930) This Republican president proposed marriage via cable telegraph from Australia to his girlfriend, Lou Henry, in California. Name him.

(931) Which president married Elizabeth Anne Bloomer on October 15, 1948 in Grand Rapids, Michigan?

REPUBLICAN TOP 10		
Most Conservative Representative		
	REPRESENTATIVE	SCORE
t1	Franks, Trent, R-Ariz.-2	93.3
t1	Shadegg, John, R-Ariz.-3	93.3
t1	Lamborn, Doug, R-Colo.-5	93.3
t1	Gingrey, Phil, R-Ga.-11	93.3
t1	Linder, John, R-Ga.-7	93.3
t1	Westmoreland, Lynn, R-Ga.-3	93.3
t1	Boehner, John, R-Ohio-8	93.3
t1	Neugebauer, Randy, R-Texas-19	93.3
9	Conaway, Mike, R-Texas-11	92.8
t10	Foxx, Virginia, R-N.C.-5	92.3
t10	Barrett, Gresham, R-S.C.-3	92.3
Source: National Journal, 2007		

(932) Which Republican, while serving as Secretary of Commerce, reduced the work day for his subordinates from twelve hours to eight hours?

(933) Which woman claimed to have an affair with Dwight Eisenhower while serving as his aide during World War II?

(934) After leaving office, which former Republican president served as food administrator for the United States under President Franklin D. Roosevelt?

10/25/1983 ▶ On order from President Reagan, U.S. forces are deployed to Grenada to rescue American hostages.

(935) Which actor did Abraham Lincoln watch in a romantic drama called "The Marble Heart" in 1863?

(936) Which American president was born in both Ohio and Delaware?

(937) This Republican president translated Dante's poem *Inferno* while courting his wife. Name him.

(938) Which well-known leader said, "Next to the destruction of the Confederacy, the death of Abraham Lincoln was the darkest day the South has ever known"?

(939) This president was paid $50,000 by *Scribner's Magazine* for his personal accounts of big-game hunting in Africa after he returned with 296 stuffed animals of 70 different species. Name him.

(940) The mother of a Republican president died after drinking milk from a cow that had eaten poisonous mushrooms. Name her.

(941) Which future president was rejected by the United States Naval Academy for being too old and therefore attended the United States Military Academy at West Point instead?

(942) Which future Republican president served in the U.S. Army during World War II but was barred from combat due to poor eyesight?

(943) What profession did Ulysses S. Grant initially want to pursue upon graduating from the Military Academy?

(944) How many crashes did George H. W. Bush, a former naval aviator, survive during World War II?

(945) At which Ivy League university did Dwight Eisenhower serve as president from 1948 to 1950?

(946) What personal item belonging to Ulysses S. Grant did a servant girl mistakenly toss into the Mississippi River while the Union Army was besieging Vicksburg during the Civil War?

Herbert and Lou Hoover

(947) Who did Jenna Bush marry in May 2008 at the Bush family ranch in Crawford, Texas?

(948) The body of this president's father was exhumed and sold to the Ohio Medical College in Cincinnati as a training cadaver but later recovered and re-interred. Name the Republican president.

(949) Which future president collected and recycled scrap iron for extra money during his boyhood?

(950) To celebrate their silver anniversary, this presidential couple repeated their wedding vows in a White House ceremony where the first lady even wore her old wedding dress. Name this couple who had seven boys.

(951) This future Republican president participated in fifty battles and engagements during the Civil War. Name this Ohioan.

(952) Which of the following positions did Warren Harding have prior to becoming president? (a) New York attorney, (b) newspaper publisher, (c) engineer, (d) admiral

(953) Which Republican president and wife moved 27 times in 37 years?

(954) Two presidential couples share January 6 as their wedding date. George and Martha Washington, married in 1759, share the date with which Republican couple?

(955) A statue of Laddie Boy, a presidential pet dog, was created by melting down 19,134 pennies donated by paperboys. Name this president.

(956) John McCain's grandfather and father were the first to earn what military distinction?

(957) For what reason was Ulysses S. Grant nearly court-martialed in 1854 and forced to resign from the army?

(958) Prior to becoming president, George W. Bush was owner of Arbusto Energy company. What does Arbusto translate to in Spanish?

(959) From which historical figure was Richard Nixon's first name derived?

(960) During the 1930s, Dwight D. Eisenhower was an aide to a noted United States Army general for seven years. Name this general.

(961) Which distinguished Civil War leader exclaimed of Ulysses S. Grant, "I have never found Grant's superior as a general"?

(962) After whom are Jenna and Barbara Bush, the daughters of President George W. Bush, named in honor?

(963) In 2001, what did Jenna and Barbara Bush do that landed them in hot water while in Austin, Texas?

(964) Two future presidents served in the Union Army's 23rd Ohio Regiment during the Civil War. Name the two.

(965) Awarded the Silver Star, Bronze Star, and two Purple Heart medals during his service in the Vietnam War, this 1968 graduate of the United States Naval Academy is most remembered for his involvement in the Iran-Contra affair. Name this former Marine born in San Antonio.

(966) During the Civil War, which future president had four horses shot from under him while serving in the Union Army?

(967) Quentin, the son of a former Republican president and pilot with the American Expeditionary Force, was shot down and killed in a dogfight over France by German aircraft during World War I. Name the presidential father.

(968) Lucky was the name of the Reagan family's first White House pet. What breed of dog was Lucky?

4/14/1986 ▶ President Reagan orders air strikes against Libya for its role in recent terrorist activities.

(969) How many Republican presidents were lawyers before their time in the White House?

(970) Who was the only Republican president to head a labor union having been elected to six one-year terms?

(971) Steven, the son of a Republican president, was a cast member on *The Young and the Restless*. Name the presidential father.

(972) The father of this Republican was a Baptist preacher in Vermont and New York. Name the president.

(973) Which future Republican president and his wife were among 200 foreigners besieged in the city of Tientsin, China during the Boxer Rebellion in 1900?

(974) On the set of which motion picture film did Ronald Reagan propose to his first wife Jane Wyman?

(975) Which president owned a dog named veto?

(976) What was the code name for Supreme Allied Commander Dwight D. Eisenhower during World War II?

10/22/1986 ▶ President Reagan signs the Tax Reform Act, the most sweeping revision to the tax code in decades.

(977) In which motion picture film does a small girl played by famous actor Shirley Temple meet Abraham Lincoln?

(978) Which future Republican president was an Ohio lawyer who helped defend runaway slaves in court?

(979) Which future Republican president received treatment from Dr. J.P. Kellogg, a noted physician in Battle Creek, Michigan, following his complete mental breakdown at age twenty four?

(980) What became of Leon Czolgosz, assassin of President William McKinley?

(981) At which law school did Theodore Roosevelt study, even though he did not become a lawyer?

(982) While a student at Yale, this president played first base on the school's baseball team and compiled a .251 batting average in 175 at bats. Name this Republican.

(983) Which famous actor was the best man at the wedding of Ronald Reagan and Nancy Davis (Reagan)?

(984) What was Calvin Coolidge's first name by birth? (Hint: not Calvin)

(985) Which Republican president was known for eating cucumbers soaked in vinegar for breakfast?

(986) Only one Republican was a widower and not married during his time in office. Name him.

(987) This Republican, the only president to weight over 300 pounds, was the heavyweight wrestling champion at Yale for two years. Name him.

(988) Which future Republican president barely satisfied the height requirement for admission to West Point because he only stood 5'1" tall when he entered the academy?

(989) This superstitious president often carried three coins with him for good luck—a silver dollar, a French franc, and a five-guinea gold coin. Name him.

(990) Henry Fonda played the role of Abraham Lincoln in which 1939 motion picture film?

(991) The daughter of a Republican president held her senior prom at the White House. Name this daughter.

(992) Which four Republican presidents were known by names different from their birth names?

(993) Which former Republican president wrote with his left hand even though he was right handed?

(994) Which 20th-century Republican president was orphaned at a young age and raised by relatives in Iowa and Oregon?

(995) Which former president's daughter married Nicholas Longworth, future Speaker of the House, in a White House ceremony?

(996) At age 15, this future Republican president nearly lost his leg to amputation in order to stop blood poisoning contracted in that leg. Name him.

(997) This president used his own money to pay for a special telegraph from the White House to his mother's home in Ohio due to her failing health. Name this president.

(998) What name did Union General Ulysses S. Grant give his horse?

1/20/1989 ▶ George H. W. Bush is inaugurated as the 41st President of the United States.

(999) This registered-Republican comedian has flown on *Air Force One*, spoken at Republican fund raisers, co-anchored *Monday Night Football*, and popularized the phrase "I am OUTTA here" while on *Saturday Night Live*. Name him.

(1000) Which Republican president was chased around by his wife with a broom?

(1001) Which Republican and Civil War general from Ohio said, "The manner by which women are treated is a good criterion to judge the true state of society"?

2/22/1989 ▶ Lieutenant Colonel Oliver North is tried for his alleged involvement in the Iran-Contra affair.

Republican National Convention, 1920

CHANTER

ANSWERS

"Far and away the best prize that life offers is the chance to work hard at work worth doing."

- THEODORE ROOSEVELT

"Lincoln had faith in time, and time has justified his faith."

- BENJAMIN HARRISON

Chapter 1

(1) Whig Party

(2) Thomas Jefferson

(3) Republican National Committee (RNC)

(4) Gettysburg battlefield in Pennsylvania

(5) John Birch Society

(6) Crater Lake National Park

(7) Stephen A. Douglas

(8) Richard Nixon

(9) Ford's Theater

(10) Moon landing in 1969

(11) Christian Coalition

(12) Hannibal Hamlin, under Abraham Lincoln

(13) Theodore & Edith Roosevelt (Theodore Roosevelt Sanctuary & Audubon Center)

(14) Chicago (in Lincoln Park)

(15) Jackson, Michigan

(16) Lincoln head penny

(17) George H. W. Bush

(18) Ann Arbor, Michigan

(19) Parthenon in Athens, Greece

(20) Ronald Reagan Washington National Airport

(21) Abraham Lincoln

(22) Brazil

(23) James Garfield

(24) National Federation of Republican Women

(25) North Dakota

(26) Lincoln Memorial Reflecting Pool

(27) Chicago (Grant Park)

(28) Grand Rapids, Michigan

(29) Gay and lesbian

(30) Calvin Coolidge Presidential Library and Museum

(31) (b) 1876

(32) Indianapolis, IN

(33) Eagle

(34) John C. Fremont

(35) States of the Union at the time of Lincoln's assassination in 1865

(36) Springfield, Illinois

(37) Gettysburg Address and Second Inaugural Address

(38) Lincoln Memorial

(39) General Grant National Memorial ("Grant's Tomb")

(40) Homeland Security

(41) St. Louis, Missouri

(42) Nevada

(43) Illinois

(44) Calvin Coolidge (nicknamed "Silent Cal")

(45) Nimitz-class nuclear-powered supercarrier

(46) (c) 24%

(47) Texas A&M University

(48) Republican National Committee

(49) Abilene, Kansas

(50) Ronald Reagan Presidential Library

(51) (a) 1888

(52) Hoover Dam

(53) Red

(54) The Washington Hilton

(55) George H. W. Bush

(56) Expansion of slavery into Kansas

(57) Kentucky

(58) Grand Old Party

(59) Lincoln Day

(60) Young Republicans

(61) Galena

(62) None, red is the unofficial color

(63) $5 bill

(64) Long Island, New York

(65) The Vietnam Veterans Memorial

(66) The Moral Majority

(67) National Union Party (for the 1864 elections)

(68) (d) 55 million

(69) Robert E. Lee's

(70) Theodore Roosevelt Island

(71) Lincoln Memorial

(72) Elephant

(73) Rutherford Hayes

(74) Ohio

(75) Ripon, Wisconsin

(76) Lincoln, Nebraska

Chapter 2

(77) William H. Taft

(78) Abraham Lincoln, on the 1909 penny

(79) Gerald Ford

(80) Dwight D. Eisenhower

(81) (c) 1894

(82) Newton Leroy "Newt" Gingrich

(83) Robert Mathias, in 1948 and 1952

(84) Great White Fleet

(85) George H. W. Bush

(86) William McKinley

(87) Ronald Reagan

(88) Herbert Hoover

(89) First women to serve in a state legislature in U.S. history

(90) Dwight D. Eisenhower

(91) Ileana Ros-Lehtinen

(92) Lucy Hayes, wife of Rutherford B. Hayes

(93) Theodore Roosevelt

(94) Twelve, and all controlled by Republicans

(95) Benjamin and Caroline Harrison, in 1889

(96) Operation Overlord

(97) Chester A. Arthur (GOP nominated James G. Blaine)

(98) Gerald Ford

(99) Bureau of the Budget

(100) Self-government

(101) 2000 & 2004

(102) Nancy Kassebaum

(103) Abraham Lincoln, in 1862

(104) Dwight D. Eisenhower

Ultimate Republican Trivia

2/27/1991 ► President Bush declares the liberation of Kuwait and defeat of Iraq.

(105) Nobel Peace Prize

(106) Federal Deposit Insurance Corporation (FDIC)

(107) Margaret Chase Smith

(108) First Hispanic-American senator

(109) Marion E. Martin

(110) Dwight D. Eisenhower

(111) George H. W. Bush

(112) Chester Arthur

(113) Rutherford B. Hayes, in the late 1870s

(114) Theodore Roosevelt

(115) Ronald Reagan (nominated Sandra Day O'Connor)

(116) Veterans Affairs

(117) Dwight D. Eisenhower

(118) Mary Lincoln

(119) Dwight D. Eisenhower

(120) Piyush "Bobby" Jindal, born in 1971

(121) George H. W. Bush, both in 1990

(122) Dwight D. Eisenhower, in 1955

(123) Herbert Hoover

(124) Distinguished Flying Cross

(125) Abraham Lincoln

(126) William Howard Taft, in 1910

(127) Gerald Ford, in 1973

(128) James Hayes (Spanish-American War), son of Rutherford B. Hayes and Theodore Roosevelt, Jr. (World War II), son of Theodore Roosevelt, Sr.

(129) Abraham Lincoln

(130) Estelle Reel

(131) George W. Bush

(132) Dwight D. Eisenhower

(133) Herbert Hoover

(134) Honorary knighthood

(135) Equal Suffrage Amendment

(136) Dwight Eisenhower, in 1956

(137) Rutherford B. Hayes

(138) Herbert Hoover

(139) First president to visit the West Coast

(140) Herbert Hoover (lived 90 years and 72 days)

(141) Theodore Roosevelt

(142) Romualdo Pacheco

(143) Calvin Coolidge (sesquicentennial half-dollar coin in 1926)

(144) Theodore Roosevelt

(145) Abraham Lincoln

(146) Richard Nixon, who was 40

(147) Richard "Dick" Cheney

(148) Warren Harding, in 1920

(149) Jeannette Rankin

(150) Benjamin Harrison

(151) Herbert Hoover (Hooveria in 1920)

(152) Ronald Reagan, in 1981

(153) Homestead Act

(154) Clare Booth Luce

(155) Richard Nixon

(156) Abraham Lincoln, in 1863

(157) Ulysses S. Grant

2/1/1992 ► **Russian leader Boris Yeltsin and President Bush declare an end to the Cold War.**

(158) Dwight D. Eisenhower

(159) Benjamin Harrison

(160) Nebraska

(161) Abraham Lincoln and Theodore Roosevelt

(162) Linda Lingle, born Linda Cutter

(163) Benjamin Harrison

(164) Melquíades Rafael "Mel" Martínez

(165) Benjamin Harrison

(166) Rudolph Giuliani

(167) Henry Kissinger

(168) Warren G. Harding

(169) Rush Limbaugh III

(170) North Dakota

(171) Elaine Chao

(172) Bertha K. Landes

(173) Richard Nixon

(174) William Howard Taft

(175) Herbert Hoover

(176) Lieutenant General

(177) Theodore Roosevelt

(178) Alexander Graham Bell

(179) First African-American member of the U.S. House of Representatives

(180) Rudolph Giuliani

(181) Hawaiian islands

(182) Ronald Reagan

(183) Patricia Fukuda "Pat" Saiki

(184) George H. W. Bush

(185) Rutherford B. Hayes, in 1878

(186) Pinckney Benton Stewart Pinchback

(187) *Explorer I*

(188) Yellowstone National Park

(189) Ronald Reagan, in 1984

(190) Abraham Lincoln

(191) Theodore Roosevelt

(192) Thanksgiving

(193) Native Americans

(194) William McKinley (Mt. McKinley)

(195) Herbert Hoover

(196) That no government in the United States may prevent a citizen from voting based on race, color, or previous condition of servitude

(197) James Garfield

(198) Consuelo Bailey

(199) Fiorello Henry LaGuardia (1882 - 1947)

(200) Richard M. Nixon

(201) Two (1980 and 1983)

(202) Calvin Coolidge, born in 1872

(203) North American Free Trade Agreement (NAFTA)

(204) Abraham Lincoln, near Hodgenville, Kentucky

(205) Theodore Roosevelt, he became president after the assassination of President William McKinley

(206) Heather Wilson

(207) Theodore Roosevelt

(208) Herbert Hoover, born in Iowa

(209) George H. W. Bush

(210) First federal bird reservation

(211) Theodore Roosevelt

(212) Youngest naval aviator at that time

(213) Richard Nixon (Henry Kissinger shared the 1972 recognition)

(214) National Monuments Act

(215) Arnold Schwarzenegger

(216) Dwight D. Eisenhower

(217) Peace treaty that ended the Russo-Japanese War

(218) Hiram Fong

(219) Theodore Roosevelt, in 1903

(220) Gerald R. Ford

Chapter 3

(221) Zero, Lincoln was the first

(222) Richard Nixon

(223) West Virginia (1863) and Nevada (1864)

(224) Tennessee

(225) James A. Garfield

(226) Ulysses S. Grant, Herbert Hoover, and Dwight D. Eisenhower

(227) Herbert Hoover

(228) Calvin Coolidge

(229) Herbert Hoover

(230) Theodore Roosevelt

(231) Ulysses S. Grant

(232) Theodore Roosevelt

(233) Warren Harding

(234) Presbyterian

(235) California

(236) Abraham Lincoln

(237) Ronald Reagan

(238) Calvin Coolidge

(239) Egypt

(240) Theodore "Teddy" Roosevelt

(241) Cuba

(242) Theodore Roosevelt

(243) Only four—Grant, Eisenhower, Reagan, and Bush, Jr.

(244) Nicaragua

(245) Jimmy Hoffa

(246) Calvin Coolidge

(247) Abraham Lincoln

(248) Bert

(249) Dwight D. Eisenhower

(250) Winston Churchill

(251) Dwight D. Eisenhower, in 1954

(252) Oklahoma

(253) Gerald R. Ford

(254) Leonid Brezhnev

(255) Ronald Reagan

(256) Dwight D. Eisenhower

(257) Ronald Reagan

(258) Richard Nixon

(259) Ronald Reagan

(260) Nelson A. Rockefeller

(261) Ronald Reagan

(262) 'W', in reference to his middle name

(263) Poker with whiskey and cigars

12/3/1993 ▶ **President Bush and Russian leader Boris Yeltsin sign the Strategic Arms Reduction Treaty (START-II).**

(264) Chester Arthur

(265) William Howard Taft

(266) George W. Bush

(267) William Howard Taft

(268) Richard Nixon, in August 1974

(269) Wrote Latin with one hand and Greek with the other hand

(270) Ronald Reagan

(271) Ulysses S. Grant

(272) Muammar al-Qaddafi

(273) All shootings took place in odd numbered years—1865, 1881, 1901, and 1981

(274) Theodore Roosevelt

(275) Dominican Republican

(276) Eisenhower Doctrine

(277) Richard Nixon

(278) Harry S. Truman

(279) Jerry Ford

(280) Benjamin Harrison

(281) George W. Bush

(282) Ulysses S. Grant

(283) Ronald Reagan

(284) President Theodore Roosevelt

(285) Alaska and Hawaii

(286) 600 Ship Navy

(287) Dwight D. Eisenhower, in 1955

(288) Chester Arthur and Gerald Ford

(289) William McKinley

(290) Ronald Reagan

(291) Theodore Roosevelt (daughter Alice)

(292) Ronald Reagan

(293) The Nixons

(294) Gerald Ford

(295) John Wilkes Booth (assassin of Lincoln)

(296) Reaganomics

(297) South East Asia Treaty Organization (SEATO)

(298) Warren Gamaliel Harding

(299) James Garfield

(300) James Garfield (assassinated), Chester Arthur (finished Garfield's term), Warren Harding (died in office), and Gerald Ford (finished Richard Nixon's term after resigning)

(301) William Howard Taft

(302) Abraham Lincoln

(303) Theodore Roosevelt

(304) Desert Shield and Desert Storm

(305) Theodore Roosevelt

(306) Ku Klux Klan

(307) Chester Arthur

(308) Warren G. Harding

(309) Somalia

(310) Savings and loan (S&L)

(311) Ronald Reagan (joking after being shot in 1981)

(312) Cuba

(313) Dwight Eisenhower

(314) Dwight D. Eisenhower

(315) Ronald Reagan

(316) Calvin Coolidge, in 1925

(317) Theodore Roosevelt

(318) Rutherford B. Hayes

(319) Theodore Roosevelt

(320) Ronald Reagan

(321) Theodore Roosevelt

(322) Calvin Coolidge

(323) Camp David

(324) District of Columbia

(325) (b) 16th

(326) Chester Arthur

(327) Supply-side economics

(328) Arizona and New Mexico

(329) William McKinley

(330) Secretary of State Henry Kissinger

(331) Alice Roosevelt, daughter of Theodore Roosevelt

(332) Abe

(333) Crown of his stovepipe hat

(334) Approximately two minutes

(335) Ronald Reagan

(336) Dwight David Eisenhower, born David Dwight Eisenhower

(337) Calvin Coolidge

(338) Colorado

(339) Gerald R. Ford, filled in for Spiro Agnew and then Richard Nixon

(340) William Howard Taft

(341) Air traffic controllers

(342) Ulysses S. Grant

(343) Theodore Roosevelt, who said, "That coffee tastes good, even to the last drop."

(344) Richard Nixon

(345) Ronald Reagan

(346) Chester Arthur

(347) Theodore Roosevelt

(348) Chester Arthur

(349) Gerald Ford

(350) William Howard Taft

(351) Star Wars

(352) Ten-mile-wide canal zone in Panama

(353) Dwight Eisenhower

(354) Queen Elizabeth II

(355) Ronald Reagan

(356) Abraham Lincoln, in the Gettysburg Address

(357) Theodore Roosevelt

(358) Tricky Dickie

(359) Ronald Reagan (occurred in a movie shoot)

(360) Australia

(361) Communism

(362) Rutherford Hayes (termed ended), James Garfield (assassinated), and Chester Arthur (vice president who became president)

(363) Theodore Roosevelt, TR

(364) Iva Toguri D' Aquino (Tokyo Rose)

(365) Confederate $5 bill

(366) Russian launch of Sputnik

(367) (d) 1974

(368) William Howard Taft

(369) Marfan's syndrome

11/8/1994 ▶ **The Republican Party gains control of both houses of Congress for the first time in four decades.**

(370) Fidel Castro, in 1985

(371) Shock and Awe

(372) Calvin Coolidge

(373) Gerald R. Ford

(374) Gerald Ford

(375) Only two

(376) Alzheimer's

(377) Postmaster General

(378) Calvin Coolidge

(379) 46th

(380) Spain

(381) Chile

(382) Theodore Roosevelt, in 1906 to inspect work on the Panama Canal

(383) Richard Nixon

(384) Gerald R. Ford

(385) Dwight Eisenhower

(386) Panama Canal

(387) General Manuel Noriega

(388) Pardoning of Richard Nixon

(389) Ronald Reagan

(390) Hippies

(391) Dwight D. Eisenhower

(392) Chester Arthur, Theodore Roosevelt, Calvin Coolidge, and Gerald Ford

(393) Theodore Roosevelt

(394) Herbert Hoover

(395) Major George S. Patton (under the overall command of General Douglas MacArthur)

(396) Strategic Arms Reduction Treaty, or Start II

(397) Theodore Roosevelt

(398) Iraq, Iran, and North Korea

(399) New York City

(400) Theodore Roosevelt

(401) Benjamin Harrison

Chapter 4

(402) J. Edgar Hoover

(403) Mr. Republican

(404) Senator Pete Domenici

(405) Press Secretary Jerry terHorst

(406) Herbert Hoover

(407) *Years of Upheaval*

(408) Alexander Haig

(409) John Paul Stevens, in 1975

(410) Colin Powell and Condoleezza Rice

(411) Edward Spencer Abraham

(412) James G. Blaine, speaker of the U.S. House of Representatives

(413) Colin Luther Powell, United States Army (Ret.)

(414) Ulysses S. Grant

(415) David H. Souter (1990) and Clarence Thomas (1991)

(416) Jesse A. Helms, Jr.

(417) Lindsey O. Graham

(418) Ervin Committee (for Senator Sam Erwin)

(419) Patriot Act

(420) Robert Bork

(421) Julius Caesar

(422) No Child Left Behind Act of 2001

(423) Peter Barton "Pete" Wilson

(424) John Chafee

(425) Central Intelligence Agency (CIA)

(426) William Tecumseh Sherman

(427) Robert Lincoln, son of Abraham Lincoln

(428) Ronald Reagan

(429) William S. Cohen

(430) Charles Evan Hughes

(431) John W. Warner III

(432) Richard Nixon

(433) Gerald Ford

(434) John Mitchell

(435) McCarthyism

(436) Harriet Ellan Miers

(437) John Ashcroft

(438) Carl Schurz (1829 – 1906)

(439) Henry Alfred Kissinger (born Heinz Alfred Kissinger)

(440) Jack Kemp

(441) Clarence Thomas

(442) Spiro T. Agnew

(443) Monetary benefits to military veterans

(444) Dennis Hastert of Illinois

(445) William Rehnquist

(446) J. C. Watts, Jr.

(447) John Ashcroft

(448) William "Bill" Frist

(449) Department of Justice

(450) Sandra Day O'Connor

(451) Theodore Roosevelt

(452) Antonin Scalia

(453) Three

(454) The Davis Cup

(455) Antonin Scalia

(456) Harvey Leroy "Lee" Atwater

(457) Condoleezza Rice

(458) Karl C. Rove

(459) Chester Trent Lott Sr.

(460) John Heinz III

(461) John Sununu

(462) End of military reconstruction of the former Confederate states

(463) Senator Strom Thurmond

(464) Samuel Alito

(465) Richard Green "Dick" Lugar

(466) Anita Hill

(467) Bureau of Labor (later becoming the Department of Labor)

(468) Earl Warren

(469) Secretary of Defense

(470) John Roberts

(471) Arlen Spector

(472) Shirley Temple Black

(473) Robert Dole of Kansas

(474) William H. Taft, Supreme Court chief justice and former president

(475) Colin Powell

(476) John Barrasso and Michael B. Enzi

ANSWERS

12/12/2000 ▶ United States Supreme Court orders the recount of Florida votes unlawful and stopped.

(477) John Ensign

(478) Newton Leroy "Newt" Gingrich

(479) Creation of nine Circuit Courts of Appeals

(480) William Seward, Secretary of State

(481) George P. Shultz

(482) Seward's Folly

(483) Donald Rumsfeld

Chapter 5

(484) Helen Taft

(485) Michael Dale "Mike" Huckabee

(486) Territory of Guam

(487) Grace Coolidge

(488) James Richard "Rick" Perry

(489) Smith College

(490) Varina Davis, wife of former Confederate President Jefferson Davis

(491) Grace Coolidge

(492) Marion "Pat" Robertson

(493) Mary Lincoln

(494) Mitt Romney

(495) Frederic Barnes

(496) Katherine Harris

(497) John Connally

(498) Frank D. Stella

(499) John "Jeb" Bush

(500) Caroline Harrison (wife of Benjamin Harrison)

(501) Mary Todd Lincoln

(502) Richard "Rick" Santorum

(503) John Ellis "Jeb" Bush

(504) William Kristol

(505) *The O'Reilly Factor*

(506) Katherine Harris

(507) Thelma "Pat" Nixon

(508) James Clayton "Jim" Dobson

(509) Willard

(510) Massachusetts

(511) Arnold Schwarzenegger

(512) James Danforth "Dan" Quayle

(513) Rudolph Giuliani

(514) Laura Bush, wife of George W. Bush

(515) Laura Bush

(516) Spiro T. Agnew

(517) Kitty Kelley

(518) Robert Lincoln, son of Abraham Lincoln

(519) Thomas "Tom" Ridge

(520) Mary Louise Smith

(521) Mamie Eisenhower

(522) Elizabeth Dole, of Kansas

(523) Henry L. Stimson (Secretary of War) and Frank Knox (Secretary of the Navy)

(524) Piano

(525) Lou Hoover

(526) Silver Fox

(527) Theodore Roosevelt, Jr.

(528) George Felix Allen

(529) Margaret "Peggy" Noonan

1/16/2001 ▶ **Former president Theodore Roosevelt receives (posthumously) the Medal of Honor, America's highest military honor.**

(530) Mary Todd (she dated Stephen A. Douglas who ran against Abraham Lincoln in 1860)

(531) George H. W. Bush

(532) First women to be officially seated at a Republican National Convention

(533) China

(534) She had one brother and three half-brothers in the Confederate Army

(535) Ronald and Nancy Reagan

(536) Michael Bloomberg

(537) George Ervin "Sonny" Perdue III

(538) *My Turn*

(539) Lynn Curtis Swann

(540) Roderick Raynor "Rod" Paige

(541) William McKinley

(542) Nancy Reagan

(543) Barbara Bush, wife of George H. W. Bush

(544) Herbert and Lou Hoover

(545) Mabel Walker Willebrandt

(546) Nancy Reagan

(547) Haley Reeves Barbour

(548) John "Jeb" Bush

(549) Nancy Davis Reagan

(550) Curt Schilling

(551) William "Bill" Frist

(552) Nancy Reagan

(553) Conrad Burns

(554) Arizona

(555) Barbara Pierce Bush

(556) Helen Taft (planted the first one herself in 1912)

(557) Mary Todd Lincoln

(558) Secretary of Labor

(559) William Seward

(560) Paul Gigot

(561) Alberto Gonzales

(562) Senator from Connecticut

(563) Ann H. Coulter

(564) Rush Limbaugh III

(565) George Pataki

(566) Arnold Schwarzenegger

(567) Rush Limbaugh III

(568) Karl C. Rove

(569) Two actually - William Louis

(570) Charles Joseph "Charlie" Crist, Jr.

(571) Robert Lincoln, son of Abraham Lincoln

(572) Timothy LaHaye

(573) *Betty: A Glad Awakening*

(574) Grace Coolidge

(575) *Crash Landing*

(576) Betty Ford (the Betty Ford Center)

(577) Sean Patrick Hannity

(578) George W. Romney

(579) Richard "Dick" Cheney

(580) Caroline Harrison

(581) Deaf children

(582) Richard DeVos, Sr.

(583) Thelma "Pat" Nixon

1/20/2001 ▶ **George W. Bush is inaugurated as the 43rd President of the United States.**

---

(584) Lou Hoover

(585) Christine Todd "Christie" Whitman

(586) Marshall C. Sanford

(587) Michelle Malkin

(588) Ida McKinley

(589) Lou Hoover

(590) Broken leg

(591) Nancy Reagan

(592) William L. Clements

(593) Barry Goldwater

(594) Elizabeth "Betty" Bloomer Ford

(595) Barbara Bush

(596) Thelma "Pat" Nixon

(597) Lucy Hayes, wife of Rutherford B. Hayes

(598) Alan Lee Keyes

(599) Andrew Carnegie

Chapter 6

(600) (b) 5 (271 to 266)

(601) (a) 10%

(602) Dwight D. Eisenhower, on February 6, 1968

(603) Benjamin Harrison

(604) One

(605) (d) 52%

(606) Jack Kemp of Maryland

(607) John McCain

(608) Charles A. Lindbergh

(609) Progressive Party

(610) Zero

(611) Candidates that lost to Richard Nixon

(612) *Our American Cousin*

(613) George Washington

(614) Ronald Reagan

(615) (c) 57% (66% for officers)

(616) Buffalo, New York

(617) (d) 44%

(618) Richard Nixon

(619) William McKinley, in 1896 and 1900

(620) George H. W. Bush

(621) Minnesota

(622) Tomb of the Unknown Soldier

(623) Richard Nixon and Nelson Rockefeller

(624) Barry Morris Goldwater

(625) George W. Bush (spoken to Dick Cheney)

(626) Mild case of smallpox

(627) Gerald Ford

(628) Grenada

(629) John Anderson

(630) Herbert Hoover

(631) Albert Gore, Sr.

(632) Assassination of President James Garfield

(633) Alfred M. Landon

(634) Gained New Mexico and Iowa and lost New Hampshire

(635) George H. W. Bush

(636) Arizona State University

(637) *Chicago Tribune*

4/29/2001 ▶ **The Bush administration announces its plan to develop a missile defense shield.**

(638) S.S. *Mayaguez*

(639) Driving Under the Influence (DUI)

(640) Steve Forbes

(641) "I Like Ike"

(642) Governor of California

(643) Guam

(644) Operation Dixie

(645) Thomas E. Dewey (defeated by Franklin D. Roosevelt in 1944 and Harry S. Truman in 1948)

(646) (d) 23%

(647) Geraldine A. Ferraro

(648) Michael Dukakis

(649) Ricky Martin

(650) Ross Perot

(651) 2004, at Madison Square Garden

(652) Michael S. Dukakis

(653) Gerald Ford

(654) Alexander Graham Bell

(655) Adlai Stevenson

(656) Kettle Hill (during the Battle of San Juan Hill)

(657) Andrew Johnson, vice president under Lincoln

(658) Elizabeth Dole

(659) George B. McClellan

(660) Admiral Dewey

(661) Ronald Reagan, in 1982

(662) The Washington National Cathedral

(663) Ronald Reagan

(664) U.S.S. *Maine*

(665) Abraham Lincoln

(666) Richard M. Nixon

(667) Eleanor Roosevelt (to Franklin D. Roosevelt, 32nd President of the United States)

(668) Knoxville, Tennessee

(669) Ann Richards

(670) Puerto Rico

(671) Ronald Reagan

(672) George H. W. Bush

(673) Barry Goldwater

(674) Ulysses S. Grant and Rutherford B. Hayes

(675) Bush/Gore in 2000

(676) George H. W. Bush

(677) Ronald Reagan, in 1984

(678) Abraham Lincoln and James Garfield

(679) Florida (2000) and Ohio (2004)

(680) Herbert Hoover

(681) Theodore Roosevelt (but on the Progressive Party ticket)

(682) Lebanon

(683) Good Friday

(684) Ronald Reagan

(685) John Wilkes Booth (his assassin)

(686) George H. W. Bush

(687) Jimmy Carter (1980) and Walter Mondale (1984)

(688) George H. W. Bush

(689) Ford's Theater

(690) Ronald Reagan

(691) Iran

ANSWERS

6/7/2001 ► A $1.35 trillion tax-cut bill is signed by President Bush.

(692) Ulysses S. Grant

(693) *Leadership 1980*

(694) Richard Nixon

(695) 1980

(696) George H. W. Bush

(697) Warren Harding

(698) U-2

(699) Julie Nixon (daughter of Richard Nixon) and David Eisenhower (grandson of Dwight D. Eisenhower)

(700) Press Secretary James Brady

(701) Al Gore, Ralph Nader, and Pat Buchanan

(702) Andrew Johnson

(703) Abraham Lincoln

(704) (a) 15%

(705) States' Rights Party

(706) Gerald Ford

(707) James A. Garfield of Ohio in 1880

(708) Julia Grant, wife of Ulysses S. Grant

(709) Assassination of President William McKinley

(710) Chicago (14 in total)

(711) John W. Hinckley, Jr.

Chapter 7

(712) Suspend the 18.4 cents per gallon federal gas tax

(713) Alaska and off-shores

(714) Prescription drugs

(715) John Roberts and Samuel Alito

(716) (a) North Vietnam

(717) Scotch-Irish

(718) Internet Tax Freedom Act of 2007

(719) *Tonight Show with David Letterman*

(720) Yes

(721) In favor

(722) Virginia (Alexandria)

(723) Intelligent design

(724) Panama Canal Zone

(725) Supports

(726) Barack Obama

(727) Support, for both Roberts and Alito

(728) Cindy Lou Hensley McCain

(729) *TIME* magazine

(730) United States Marine Corps

(731) 22

(732) Supports the ban on lawsuits

(733) Crown Prince

(734) Charity

(735) True

(736) Straight Talk Express

(737) Melanoma

(738) John McCain's experiences in Vietnam

(739) Yes

(740) Commander of all U.S. forces in the Pacific

(741) For his ability to attract women

(742) (c) 2005

(743) Yes

(744) Corpus Christi Bay

(745) White Tornado

(746) A-4 Skyhawk

(747) Fiddle

(748) Ardent supporter of Israel and its government policies

(749) Yes

(750) U.S.S. *Forrestal*

(751) Robert the Bruce

(752) He himself, John McCain

(753) Economic Stimulus Package of tax rebates

(754) (c) 87

(755) Pro-Life and anti-abortion

(756) Armed Services and Indian Affairs

(757) All

(758) (b) 1958

(759) 1982

(760) Election campaign financing

(761) Arizona

(762) Maverick

(763) Staff member for General George Washington

(764) Hold his breath until he blacked out

(765) American flag desecration

(766) Hanoi Hilton

(767) Japanese surrender of World War II

(768) Confederacy

(769) Alfalfa Club

(770) Mother Theresa

(771) Chuck Hagel of Nebraska

(772) Episcopalian

Chapter 8

(773) Ulysses S. Grant

(774) Football & boxing

(775) (d) 58

(776) Theodore Roosevelt

(777) Abraham Lincoln

(778) Poor eyesight

(779) James Garfield

(780) Herbert Hoover

(781) *Love Is on the Air*

(782) *Sic semper tyrannis*, meaning "Thus ever to tyrants" (the state motto of Virginia)

(783) Ulysses S. Grant

(784) Abraham Lincoln

(785) George H. W. Bush

(786) Barbara

(787) Vicksburg

(788) Ronald Reagan

(789) Tiffany's (perhaps not as rough as thought)

(790) James Clayton "Jim" Dobson

(791) Five

(792) Benjamin Harrison

(793) Donald "Don" King

(794) *Bedtime for Bonzo*

(795) Harry S. Truman

(796) John McCain

(797) William McKinley

(798) 12

(799) *Kissinger and Nixon*

(800) Richard Nixon

(801) Knute Rockne

(802) Abraham Lincoln (Lincoln Logs)

(803) Herbert Hoover

(804) Rancho de Cielo

(805) Gerald Ford

(806) Ronald Reagan

(807) Gerald Ford

(808) Abraham Lincoln

(809) *Looking Forward*

(810) Andy García, born Andrés Arturo García y Menéndez

(811) Lincoln Memorial

(812) Ulysses S. Grant

(813) Calvin and Grace Coolidge

(814) Ulysses S. Grant

(815) Ronald Reagan

(816) *Hellcats of the Navy*

(817) Theodore Roosevelt (occurred in 1912 while running for president on the Progressive Party ticket)

(818) Theodore Roosevelt

(819) Chester Arthur

(820) Gerald Ford

(821) Spectacles/glasses

(822) Ronald Reagan

(823) Abraham Lincoln

(824) Rutherford Birchard Hayes, Richard Milhous Nixon, Ronald Wilson Reagan, and George Herbert Walker Bush

(825) Ronald Reagan

(826) Anthony Hopkins

(827) Hiram Ulysses Grant

(828) George H. W. Bush

(829) National Rifle Association

(830) (d) 53

(831) George H. W. Bush

(832) Abraham Lincoln

(833) Dwight Eisenhower

(834) Philippines

(835) Richard Nixon

(836) David Duke

(837) John Hinckley, Jr.

(838) Gerald Ford

(839) Little Ben

(840) John Aspinwall Roosevelt

(841) He served as Secretary of War under President Theodore Roosevelt

(842) Ulysses S. Grant

(843) Gerald Ford

(844) Rubbers

(845) Theodore Roosevelt

(846) William Howard Taft

(847) Ronald Reagan

(848) Boxing

(849) Richard Nixon

(850) Abraham Lincoln

(851) Checkers

(852) The Order of Skull and Bones

(853) Broccoli

(854) Theodore Roosevelt

1/29/2002 ▶ **During his State of the Union Address, President Bush first uses the term "Axis of Evil."**

(855) Benjamin Harrison

(856) Abraham Lincoln

(857) Cocaine

(858) Richard Nixon

(859) None, all had siblings

(860) Theodore Roosevelt

(861) Adolf Hitler

(862) West Point mistakenly listed him as Ulysses Simpson Grant whereby Simpson was his mother's maiden name. The name stuck.

(863) Ronald Reagan

(864) Texas Air National Guard

(865) Abraham Lincoln

(866) George W. Bush (Yale, 1966)

(867) George H. W. Bush

(868) The Great Pyramid at Giza

(869) *Anger Management*

(870) Calvin Coolidge

(871) The squirrels were digging up the White House putting green

(872) Rutherford B. Hayes

(873) Theodore Roosevelt

(874) Massachusetts

(875) Abraham Lincoln

(876) Jellybeans

(877) George "The Gipper" Gipp

(878) George H. W. Bush

(879) Robert Bork

(880) Yale University

(881) Gloria Estefan, born Gloria María Fajardo

(882) Augusta National Golf Club

(883) William H. Vanderbilt

(884) Herbert C. Hoover, born in West Branch, Iowa

(885) Gave the slave his freedom

(886) Ronald Reagan

(887) Comics

(888) Warren G. Harding

(889) Gerald Rudolph Ford, Jr.

(890) Elvis Presley

(891) Joseph "Joe" Lieberman

(892) Benjamin Harrison

(893) Patti (Reagan) Davis, in *Playboy*

(894) Liberty

(895) Black Hawk War

(896) Eight (Lincoln, Grant, Hayes, Roosevelt, Harding, Coolidge, Ford, and Bush, Jr.)

(897) Richard Nixon

(898) Ohio (Grant, Hayes, and Garfield)

(899) Dwight D. Eisenhower

(900) *The National Review*

(901) Herbert Hoover

(902) Hearing aid

(903) Gerald Ford

(904) Chester Arthur

(905) Ohio

(906) George H. W. Bush

(907) Shooting of Ronald Reagan

(908) Abraham Lincoln

6/2/2002 ▶ **President Bush proposes the creation of the Department of Homeland Security.**

(909) German Chancellor Angela Merkel

(910) Benjamin Harrison

(911) Chester A. Arthur

(912) Oregon

(913) Dwight D. Eisenhower

(914) Theodore Roosevelt

(915) Dwight D. Eisenhower, nicknamed "Ike"

(916) Rutherford Hayes, in the Red Room

(917) Ulysses S. Grant

(918) William McKinley, in Poland, Ohio!

(919) Ulysses S. Grant

(920) William Howard Taft

(921) George W. Bush

(922) Dwight D. Eisenhower

(923) Warren Harding

(924) William McKinley

(925) Millie

(926) Theodore Roosevelt (Roosevelt Elk)

(927) Franklin D. Roosevelt

(928) Whigs

(929) Jane Wyman

(930) Herbert Hoover

(931) Gerald Ford

(932) Herbert Hoover

(933) Kay Summersby

(934) Herbert Hoover

(935) John Wilkes Booth (his assassin)

(936) Rutherford Hayes, born in Delaware, Ohio!

(937) Calvin Coolidge

(938) Jefferson Davis, Confederate president

(939) Theodore Roosevelt

(940) Nancy Hanks Lincoln, mother of Abraham Lincoln

(941) Dwight D. Eisenhower

(942) Ronald Reagan

(943) Mathematics professor

(944) Four

(945) Columbia University

(946) His false teeth

(947) Henry Hager

(948) Benjamin Harrison

(949) Herbert Hoover

(950) Rutherford and Lucy Hayes

(951) Rutherford Hayes

(952) (b) newspaper publisher

(953) Dwight and Mamie Eisenhower (attributed to his military career)

(954) George and Barbara Bush, married in 1945

(955) Warren G. Harding

(956) First pair of father/son Four-Star admirals in the United States Navy

(957) Alcohol abuse

(958) Bush

(959) King Richard I, "the Lion Hearted"

(960) Douglas MacArthur

3/20/2003 ▶ **After approval by the full Senate and upon orders from President Bush, the United States begins the invasion of Iraq.**

(961) Confederate General Robert E. Lee

(962) Their grandmothers

(963) Ordered margaritas as minors

(964) Rutherford B. Hayes and William McKinley

(965) Oliver Laurence North

(966) Rutherford B. Hayes

(967) Theodore Roosevelt

(968) Sheepdog

(969) 10 (Lincoln, Hayes, Garfield, Arthur, Harrison, McKinley, Taft, Coolidge, Nixon, and Ford)

(970) Ronald Reagan (Screen Actors Guild)

(971) Gerald Ford

(972) Chester Arthur

(973) Herbert and Lou Hoover

(974) *Brother Rat*

(975) James A. Garfield

(976) *Look*

(977) *The Littlest Rebel*

(978) Rutherford Hayes

(979) Warren G. Harding

(980) Died in the electric chair on October 29, 1901

(981) Columbia Law School

(982) George H. W. Bush

(983) William Holden

(984) John (dropped because it was also his father's first name)

(985) Ulysses S. Grant

(986) Chester Arthur

(987) William Howard Taft

(988) Ulysses S. Grant

(989) Dwight D. Eisenhower

(990) *Young Mr. Lincoln*

(991) Susan Ford

(992) Ulysses S. Grant, Calvin Coolidge, Dwight D. Eisenhower, and Gerald R. Ford

(993) Gerald Ford

(994) Herbert Hoover

(995) Theodore Roosevelt (daughter Alice)

(996) Dwight D. Eisenhower

(997) William McKinley

(998) Jefferson Davis (Confederate president)

(999) Dennis Miller

(1000) Abraham Lincoln

(1001) Benjamin Harrison

CONCLUSION

Thank you for reading and enjoying *Ultimate Republican Trivia*. As you can imagine, producing a book of this scale takes a significant amount of work, time, and resources. In consequence, I hope you enjoyed each and every trivia included in this book as well as the many educational lists and dialog boxes. It is readers such as yourself that gives me the inspiration and motivation to write books and pursue my passion.

If you are interested in including additional trivia for the next printing or the next edition, I highly encourage you to contact me via telephone or email. Your comments on what you thought about the book are also very much welcome. Thank you again.

Cordially Yours,
Scott Frush

CONTACT INFORMATION

Scott Paul Frush
P.O. Box 1849
Royal Oak, Michigan 48068-1849

Phone: (248) 642-6800
Email: Scott@Frush.com

APPENDIX A: REPUBLICAN RESOURCES

REPUBLICAN ORGANIZATIONS

REPUBLICAN NATIONAL COMMITTEE
310 First Street
Washington, DC 20003

(202) 863-8500
www.gop.com

NATIONAL FEDERATION OF REPUBLICAN WOMEN
124 N. Alfred Street
Alexandria, VA 22314

(703) 548-9688
www.nfrw.org

COLLEGE REPUBLICAN NATIONAL COMMITTEE
600 Pennsylvania Ave. SE, Ste 215
Washington DC 20003

(888) 765-3564
www.crnc.org

NATIONAL REPUBLICAN CONGRESSIONAL COMM.
320 First Street, SE
Washington, DC 20003

(202) 479-7000
www.NRCC.org

IRISH-AMERICAN REPUBLICANS
1350 I Street, NW, Suite 200
Washington, DC 20005

www.irishrepub.org

REPUBLICAN JEWISH COALITION
50 F Street, NW, Suite 100
Washington, DC 20001

(202) 638-6688
www.rjchq.org

NATIONAL REPUBLICAN SENATORIAL COMMITTEE
425 2nd Street, NE
Washington, DC 20002

(202) 675-6000
www.nrsc.org

REPUBLICAN GOVERNORS ASSOCIATION
1747 Pennsylvania Ave., NW
Ste 250
Washington, DC 20006

(202) 662-4140
www.rga.org

REPUBLICAN NATIONAL HISPANIC ASSEMBLY
1717 Pennsylvania Avenue, NW, Suite 650
Washington, DC 20006

(202) 281-0891
www.rnha.org

NEW CENTURY PROJECT
2021 E. Dublin-Granville Road, Suite 161
Columbus, OH 43229

(614) 785-1600
www.newcenturyproject.org

NATIONAL TEEN AGE REPUBLICANS (TARS)
10620-B Crestwood Professional Ctr
Manassas, VA 20108

(703) 368-4214
www.republicanteens.org

REPUBLICAN NATIONAL LAWYERS ASSOCIATION
P.O. Box 18965
Washington, DC 20036

(703) 719-6335
www.rnla.org

NATIONAL BLACK REPUBLICAN ASSOCIATION
5824 Bee Ridge Road #419
Sarasota, FL 34233-5065

(866) 905-6701
www.nbra.info

REPUBLICANS FOR ENVIRONMENTAL PROTECTION
3200 Carlisle Blvd. NE, Suite 114
Albuquerque, NM 87110

(505) 889-4544
www.repamerica.org

REPUBLICANS ABROAD INTERNATIONAL
1275 K Street, NW, Suite 102
Washington DC, 20005

(202) 608-1423
www.republicansabroad.com

YOUNG REPUBLICAN NATIONAL FEDERATION
P.O. 15293
Washington, DC 2003-0293

(202) 608-1417
www.yrnf.com

**NATIONAL REPUBLICAN
CLUB OF CAPITOL HILL**
300 First Street, SE
Washington, DC 20003

(202) 484-4590
www.capitolhillclub.org

**REPUBLICAN NATIONAL
COALITION FOR LIFE**
P.O. 618
Alton, IL 62002

(214) 559-4460
www.rnclife.org

**REPUBLICAN LIBERTY
CAUCUS**
44 Summerfield Street
Thousand Oaks, CA 91350

(866) 752-5423
www.rlc.org

OTHER ORGANIZATIONS

**THE AMERICAN
CONSERVATIVE UNION**
1007 Cameron Street
Alexandria, VA 22314

(703) 836-8602
www.conservative.org

**THE AMERICAN
ENTERPRISE INSTITUTE**
1150 Seventeenth Street, NW
Washington, DC 20036

(202) 862-5800
www.aei.org

**AMERICANS FOR TAX
REFORM**
1920 L Street NW, Suite 200
Washington, DC 20036

(202) 785-0266
www.atr.org

**AMERICANS FOR
PROSPERITY**
1726 M Street, NW, 10th Floor
Washington, DC 20036

(866) 730-0150
www.americansforprosperity.org

GOPAC

1101 16th Street, NW, Suite 201
Washington, DC 20036

(202) 464-5170
www.gopac.org

**COALITION ON URBAN
RENEWAL AND EDUCATION**

1300 Pennsylvania Ave. NW, Ste 700
Washington, DC 20004

(202) 204-2575
www.urbancure.org

AMERICAN VALUES
P.O. Box 96192
Washington, DC 20090

(703) 671-9700
www.ouramericanvalues.org

FREEDOMWORKS
601 Pennsylvania Ave. NW, Ste 700
Washington, DC 20004

(202) 783-3870
http://www.cse.org/

**THE AMERICAN
CONSERVATIVE UNION**
1007 Cameron Street
Alexandria, VA 22314

(800) 752-4391
www.cpac.org

**THE HERITAGE
FOUNDATION**
214 Massachusetts Ave, NE
Washington DC 20002

(202) 546-4400
www.heritage.org

**THE LEADERSHIP
INSTITUTE**
1101 North Highland Street
Arlington, VA 22201

(703) 247-2000
www.leadershipinstitute.org

**NATIONAL TAXPAYERS
UNION & NTUF**
108 North Alfred Street
Alexandria, VA 22314

(703) 683-5700
www.ntu.org

Republican Presidents of the United States

No.	Name	State of Birth	Life Dates	Dates of Term	Age at Inauguration	Religion	School
16	Abraham Lincoln	Kentucky	1809-1865	1861-1865	52	No formal affiliation	None
18	Ulysses Simpson Grant	Ohio	1822-1885	1869-1877	46	Methodist	U.S. Military Academy
19	Rutherford Birchard Hayes	Ohio	1822-1893	1877-1881	54	No formal affiliation	Kenyon
20	James Abram Garfield	Ohio	1831-1881	1881	49	Disciples of Christ	Williams
21	Chester Alan Arthur	Vermont	1829-1886	1881-1885	51	Episcopalian	Union
23	Benjamin Harrison	Ohio	1833-1901	1889-1893	55	Presbyterian	Miami (Oh.)
25	William McKinley	Ohio	1843-1901	1897-1901	54	Methodist	Allegheny College
26	Theodore Roosevelt	New York	1858-1919	1901-1909	42	Dutch Reformed	Harvard
27	William Howard Taft	Ohio	1857-1930	1909-1913	51	Unitarian	Yale
29	Warren Gamaliel Harding	Ohio	1865-1923	1921-1923	55	Baptist	Ohio Central College
30	Calvin Coolidge	Vermont	1872-1933	1923-1929	51	Congregationalist	Amherst
31	Herbert Clark Hoover	Iowa	1874-1964	1929-1933	54	Quaker	Stanford
34	Dwight David Eisenhower	Texas	1890-1969	1953-1961	62	Presbyterian	U.S. Military Academy
37	Richard Milhous Nixon	California	1913-1994	1969-1974	56	Quaker	Whittier
38	Gerald Rudolph Ford, Jr.	Nebraska	1913-2006	1974-1977	61	Episcopalian	Michigan
40	Ronald Reagan	Illinois	1911-2004	1981-1989	69	Disciples of Christ	Eureka
41	George Hebert Walker Bush	Massachusetts	1924-	1989-1993	64	Episcopalian	Yale
43	George Walker Bush	Connecticut	1946-	2001-2009	55	United Methodist	Yale & Harvard
44	John Sidney McCain III	Panama Canal Zone	1936-	2009-2017	73	Baptist	U.S. Naval Academy

Republican Vice Presidents of the United States

No.	Name	State of Birth	Life Dates	Dates of Term	President Served
15	Hannibal Hamlin	Maine	1809-1891	1861-1865	Abraham Lincoln
17	Schuyler Colfax	New York	1823-1885	1869-1873	Ulysses S. Grant
18	Henry Wilson	New Hampshire	1812-1875	1873-1875	Ulysses S. Grant
19	William A. Wheeler	New York	1819-1887	1877-1881	Rutherford B. Hayes
20	Chester A. Arthur	Vermont	1830-1886	1881	James A. Garfield
22	Levi P. Morton	Vermont	1824-1920	1889-1893	Benjamin Harrison
24	Garrett A. Hobart	New Jersey	1844-1899	1897-1899	William McKinley
25	Theodore Roosevelt	New York	1858-1919	1901	William McKinley
26	Charles W. Fairbanks	Ohio	1852-1918	1905-1909	Theodore Roosevelt
27	James S. Sherman	New York	1855-1912	1909-1912	William H. Taft
29	Calvin Coolidge	Vermont	1872-1933	1921-1923	Warren G. Harding
30	Charles G. Dawes	Ohio	1865-1951	1925-1929	Calvin Coolidge
31	Charles Curtis	Kansas	1860-1936	1929-1933	Herbert Hoover
36	Richard M. Nixon	California	1913-1994	1953-1961	Dwight D. Eisenhower
39	Spiro T. Agnew	Maryland	1918-1996	1969-1973	Richard M. Nixon
40	Gerald R. Ford	Nebraska	1913-2006	1973-1974	Richard M. Nixon
41	Nelson A. Rockefeller	Maine	1908-1979	1974-1977	Gerald R. Ford
43	George H. W. Bush	Massachusetts	1924-	1981-1989	Ronald Reagan
44	J. Danforth Quayle	Indiana	1947-	1989-1993	George H. W. Bush
46	Richard Cheney	Nebraska	1941-	2001-2009	George W. Bush
47	TBD	---	---	2009-2017	John McCain

Republican First Ladies of the United States

First Lady	President	State of Birth	Life Dates	Date of Marriage
Mary Todd	Abraham Lincoln	Kentucky	1818-1882	1842
Julia Dent	Ulysses S. Grant	Missouri	1826-1902	1848
Lucy Ware Webb	Rutherford B. Hayes	Ohio	1831-1889	1852
Lucretia Rudolph	James A. Garfield	Ohio	1832-1918	1858
Ellen Lewis Herdon	Chester A. Arthur	Virginia	1837-1880	1859
Caroline Lavinia Scott	Benjamin Harrison	Ohio	1832-1892	1853
Mary Scott Lord Dimmick	Benjamin Harrison	Pennsylvania	1858-1948	1896
Ida Saxton	William McKinley	Ohio	1847-1907	1871
Alice Hathaway Lee	Theodore Roosevelt	Massachusetts	1861-1884	1880
Edith Kermit Carow	Theodore Roosevelt	Connecticut	1861-1948	1886
Helen Herron	William Howard Taft	Ohio	1861-1943	1886
Florence Kling De Wolfe	Warren G. Harding	Ohio	1860-1924	1891
Grace Anna Goodhue	Calvin Coolidge	Vermont	1879-1957	1905
Lou Henry	Herbert C. Hoover	Iowa	1875-1944	1899
Mamie Geneva Doud	Dwight D. Eisenhower	Iowa	1896-1979	1916
Thelma Catherine Patricia Ryan	Richard M. Nixon	Nevada	1912-1993	1940
Elizabeth "Betty" Bloomer Warren	Gerald R. Ford, Jr.	Illinois	1918-	1948
Nancy Davis	Ronald Reagan	New York	1921-	1952
Barbara Pierce	George H. W. Bush	New York	1925-	1945
Laura Lane Welch	George W. Bush	Texas	1946-	1977
Cindy Lou Hensley	*John S. McCain III*	*Arizona*	*1954-*	*1980*

Republican Presidential and Vice Presidential Nominees

Year	Republican President	Republican Vice President	WINNER	Major Opponent President	Major Opponent Vice President
1856	John Freemont	William Dayton	►	James Buchanan	John Breckinridge
1860	Abraham Lincoln	Hannibal Hamlin	◄	John Breckinridge	Joseph Lane
1864	Abraham Lincoln	Andrew Johnson*	◄	George McClellan	G. H. Pendleton
1868	Ulysses S. Grant	Schuyler Colfax	◄	Horatio Seymour	Francis Blair
1872	Ulysses S. Grant	Henry Wilson	◄	Horace Greeley	B. Gratz Brown
1876	Rutherford B. Hayes	William Wheeler	◄	Samuel J. Tilden	Thomas Hendricks
1880	James A. Garfield	Chester A. Arthur	◄	Winfield Hancock	William English
1884	James Blaine	John Logan	►	Grover Cleveland	Thomas Hendricks
1888	Benjamin Harrison	Levi Morton	◄	Grover Cleveland	A. G. Thurman
1892	Benjamin Harrison	Whitelaw Reid	►	Grover Cleveland	Adlai Stevenson
1896	William McKinley	Garret Hobart	◄	William J. Bryan	Adlai Stevenson
1900	William McKinley	Theodore Roosevelt	◄	William J. Bryan	Adlai Stevenson
1904	Theodore Roosevelt	Charles Fairbanks	◄	Alton Parker	Henry Davis
1908	William H. Taft	James Sherman	◄	William J. Bryan	John Kern
1912	William H. Taft	James Sherman	►	Woodrow Wilson	Thomas Marshall
1916	Charles Hughes	Charles Fairbanks	►	Woodrow Wilson	Thomas Marshall
1920	Warren G. Harding	Calvin Coolidge	◄	James M. Cox	Franklin D. Roosevelt
1924	Calvin Coolidge	Charles G. Dawes	◄	John W. Davis	Charles W. Bryan
1928	Herbert Hoover	Charles Curtis	◄	Alfred E. Smith	Joseph T. Robinson
1932	Herbert Hoover	Charles Curtis	►	Franklin D. Roosevelt	John N. Garner
1936	Alfred M. Landon	Frank Knox	►	Franklin D. Roosevelt	John N. Garner
1940	Wendell L. Willkie	Charles McNary	►	Franklin D. Roosevelt	Henry A. Wallace
1944	Thomas E. Dewey	John E. Bricker	►	Franklin D. Roosevelt	Harry S. Truman
1948	Thomas E. Dewey	Earl Warren	►	Harry S. Truman	Alben W. Barkley
1952	Dwight D. Eisenhower	Richard M. Nixon	◄	Adlai E. Stevenson	John J. Sparkman
1956	Dwight D. Eisenhower	Richard M. Nixon	◄	Adlai E. Stevenson	Estes Kefauver
1960	Richard M. Nixon	Henry Cabot Lodge	►	John F. Kennedy	Lyndon B. Johnson
1964	Barry M. Goldwater	William E. Miller	►	Lyndon B. Johnson	Hubert H. Humphrey
1968	Richard M. Nixon	Spiro T. Agnew	◄	Hubert H. Humphrey	Edmund S. Muskie
1972	Richard M. Nixon	Spiro T. Agnew	◄	George S. McGovern	R. Sargent Shriver Jr.
1976	Gerald R. Ford	Robert J. Dole	►	Jimmy Carter	Walter F. Mondale
1980	Ronald Reagan	George H. W. Bush	◄	Jimmy Carter	Walter F. Mondale
1984	Ronald Reagan	George H. W. Bush	◄	Walter F. Mondale	Geraldine Ferraro
1988	George H. W. Bush	J. Danforth Quayle	◄	Michael S. Dukakis	Lloyd Bentsen
1992	George H. W. Bush	J. Danforth Quayle	►	William J. Clinton	Albert Gore, Jr.
1996	Robert J. Dole	Jack Kemp	►	William J. Clinton	Albert Gore, Jr.
2000	George W. Bush	Richard Cheney	◄	Albert Gore, Jr.	Joseph Lieberman
2004	George W. Bush	Richard Cheney	◄	John F. Kerry	John Edwards
2008	John S. McCain III	TBD	◄	Barack Hussein Obama, Jr.	TBD

* Not a Republican

BIBLIOGRAPHY

❖ ANDERSON, DALE, *The Republican Party: The Story of the Grand Old Party*, Minneapolis: Compass Point Books, 2007

❖ BARONE, MICHAEL and COHEN, RICHARD E., *The Almanac of American Politics*, Washington, D.C.: National Journal Group, 2007

❖ BOLLER, PAUL, *Presidential Campaigns*, New York: Oxford University Press, 1996

❖ BONADIO, FELICE A., *Political Parties in American History*, New York: Putnam's, 1974

❖ COUCH, ERNIE, *Presidential Trivia*, Nashville: Rutledge Hill Press, 1996

❖ DEGREGORIO, WILLIAM A., *The Complete Book of U.S. Presidents*, New York: Gramercy Books, 2005

❖ FINAMORE, FRANK, *Washington, D.C. Trivia Fact Book*, New York: Gramercy Books, 2001

❖ FONER, ERIC, *Free Soil, Free Labor, Free Men: The Ideology of the Republican Party Before the Civil War*, New York: Oxford University Press, 1970

❖ GIENAPP, WILLIAM E., *The Origins of the Republican Party, 1852-1856*, New York: Oxford University Press, 1987

❖ HUMES, JAMES C., *Which President Killed a Man?*, Chicago: Contemporary Books, 2002

❖ LANG, J. STEPHEN, *The Complete Book of Presidential Trivia*, Gretna, LA: Pelican Publishing Company, 2001

❖ LINDOP, EDMUND, *All About Republicans*, Hillsdale, NJ: Enslow Publishers, 1985

❖ MATUZ, ROGER, *The Presidents Fact Book*, New York: Black Dog & Leventhal, 2004

❖ MCGUINESS, COLLEEN, *National Party Conventions, 1831-1988*, Washington, D.C.: Congressional Quarterly, 1991

❖ MINER, BRAD, *The Concise Conservative Encyclopedia*, New York: Free Press Paperbacks, 1996

❖ O'BRIEN, CORMAC, *Secret Lives of the First Ladies*, Philadelphia: Quirk Books, 2005

❖ O'BRIEN, CORMAC, *Secret Lives of the U.S. Presidents*, Philadelphia: Quirk Books, 2004

❖ PHILLIPS, LOUIS, *Ask Me Anything About the Presidents*, New York: Avon Books, 1994

❖ REICHLEY, A. JAMES, *The Life of the Parties: A History of American Political Parties*, New York: Free Press, 1992

❖ SMITH, CARTER, *Presidents: All You Need to Know*, Irvington, New York: Hylas Publishing, 2007

❖ STADELMANN, MARCUS, *U.S. Presidents for Dummies*, Hoboken, NJ: Wiley Publishing, 2002

❖ THE EDITORS OF CHASE'S, *Chase's Calendar of Events 2008*, New York: McGraw-Hill, 2007

ORDER FORM

Telephone Orders: (800) 431-1579

Internet Orders: www.Amazon.com **or** www.ScottFrush.com

Fax Orders: (248) 232-1501 (credit card only – please include this form)

Postal Orders: Marshall Rand Publishing
P.O. Box 1849
Royal Oak, MI 48068-1849

Make check payable to *Marshall Rand Publishing*

Ship to:

Name:_____

Address:_____

City:_____ State:_____ Zip:_____

Telephone:_____

Item:

Book: ***Ultimate Republican Trivia*** ($9.95 each) $ _____
1001 *Fun and Fascinating Facts*

Postage: 2.00

Sales Tax: (Michigan residents, add $0.60 for each book) _____

Total: (please sum) $_____

Payment: Check Visa MasterCard

Card number:_____

Name on card:_____ Exp. Date:_____

Ultimate!
REPUBLICAN
TRIVIA

To Doug